Workshop on Embodied Language Processing 2007

Held in conjunction with ACL 2007

Prague, Czech Republic
29 June 2007

ISBN: 978-1-61738-526-1

Printed from e-media with permission by:

Curran Associates, Inc.
57 Morehouse Lane
Red Hook, NY 12571

Some format issues inherent in the e-media version may also appear in this print version.

Printed by Curran Associates, Inc. (2010)

For permission requests, please contact the Association for Computational Linguistics
at the address below.

Association for Computational Linguistics
209 N. Eighth Street
Stroudsburg, Pennsylvania 18360

Phone: 1-570-476-8006
Fax: 1-570-476-0860

acl@aclweb.org

Additional copies of this publication are available from:

Curran Associates, Inc.
57 Morehouse Lane
Red Hook, NY 12571 USA
Phone: 845-758-0400
Fax: 845-758-2634
Email: curran@proceedings.com
Web: www.proceedings.com

Preface

Welcome to the ACL 2007 workshop on Embodied Natural Language. There has been a growing interest within the ACL community in extending the traditional focus on text and speech beyond the confines of natural language towards the inclusion of paralinguistic and non-verbal modes of communication, and beyond the confines of task-oriented language towards the inclusion of social and psychological variables such as attitude and affect. Studies of embodied dialogue systems, emotional expressiveness in speech, and personality detection in text are just a few examples of such research. These new extensions to computational linguistics have found a home in a number of different applications, from analysis of military videos to the development of Ambient Intelligent applications, where natural modes of interaction between humans and machines are envisioned that exploit the full bandwidth of human communication.

These studies in embodied language processing have close connections with other fields of inquiry such as Affective Computing and Embodied Conversational Agents. In all of these fields the many modalities through which we communicate besides language, such as facial expressions, gestures, and posture, play a prominent role. These and other related studies of nonverbal language processing offer complementary insights to traditional work in computational linguistics. After all, human-human communication is inherently multimodal, and unimodal spoken communication is really just an artifact of communications technology, specifically the telephone ... so surely the mechanisms of speech and language processing need to apply not just to word sequences but to natural (multimodal) human language distributed over multiple input streams (speech, hand gesture, gaze ...). It is increasingly clear that integrating the theories, models and algorithms developed in areas such as these with work in mainstream CL, will lead to a richer processing model of natural communication.

Workshop Chairs
Justine Cassell, Northwestern University
Dirk Heylen, University of Twente

Organizers

Chairs:

Justine Cassell, Northwestern University
Dirk Heylen, University of Twente

Program Committee:

Julia Hirschberg, Columbia University
Michael Johnston, AT&T Research
Anton Nijholt, University of Twente
Jon Oberlander, University of Edinburgh
Mark Steedman, University of Edinburgh
Matthew Stone, Rutgers University
David Traum, University of Southern California

Table of Contents

Conference Program

Friday, June 29, 2007

14:30–14:35 Welcome

14:35–15:00 *Comparing Rule-Based and Data-Driven Selection of Facial Displays*
Mary Ellen Foster

15:00–15:25 *Aiduti in Japanese Multi-Party Design Conversations*
Yasuhiro Katagiri

15:25–15:50 *Computing Backchannel Distributions in Multi-Party Conversations*
Dirk Heylen and Rieks op den Akker

15:50–16:15 Break

16:15–16:40 *Which Way to Turn? Guide Orientation in Virtual Way Finding*
Mark Evers, Mariët Theune and Joyce Karreman

16:40–17:05 *A "Person" in the Interface: Effects on User Perceptions of Multibiometrics*
Álvaro Hernández, Beatriz López, David Díaz, Rubén Fernández, Luis Hernández and Javier Caminero

17:05–17:30 *Coordination in Conversation and Rapport*
Justine Cassell, Alastair Gill and Paul Tepper

17:30–18:30 Demos & Poster Session

Design and Evaluation of an American Sign Language Generator
Matt Huenerfauth, Liming Zhou, Erdan Gu and Jan Allbeck

Dynamic Movement and Positioning of Embodied Agents in Multiparty Conversations
Dušan Jan and David Traum

Design and Validation of ECA Gestures to Improve Dialogue System Robustness
Beatriz López, Álvaro Hernández, David Díaz, Rubén Fernández, Luis Hernández and Doroteo Torre

Understanding RUTH: Reproducing Natural Behaviors in Conversational Animation
Matthew Stone and Insuk Oh

Situated Dialogue Processing for Human-Robot Interaction
Geert-Jan M. Kruijff, Henrik Jacobsson, Maria Staudte and Hendrik Zender

18:30 Post-Workshop Dinner & Discussion

Comparing Rule-based and Data-driven Selection of Facial Displays

Mary Ellen Foster
Informatik VI: Robotics and Embedded Systems
Technische Universität München
Boltzmannstraße 3, 85748 Garching, Germany
foster@in.tum.de

Abstract

The non-verbal behaviour of an embodied conversational agent is normally based on recorded human behaviour. There are two main ways that the mapping from human behaviour to agent behaviour has been implemented. In some systems, human behaviour is analysed, and then rules for the agent are created based on the results of that analysis; in others, the recorded behaviour is used directly as a resource for decision-making, using data-driven techniques. In this paper, we implement both of these methods for selecting the conversational facial displays of an animated talking head and compare them in two user evaluations. In the first study, participants were asked for subjective preferences: they tended to prefer the output of the data-driven strategy, but this trend was not statistically significant. In the second study, the data-driven facial displays affected the ability of users to perceive user-model tailoring in synthesised speech, while the rule-based displays did not have any effect.

1 Introduction

There is no longer any question that the production of language and its accompanying non-verbal behaviour are tightly linked (e.g., Bavelas and Chovil, 2000). The communicative functions of body language listed by Bickmore and Cassell (2005) include conversation initiation and termination, turn-taking and interruption, content elaboration and emphasis, and feedback and error correction; non-verbal behaviours that can achieve these functions include gaze modification, facial expressions, hand gestures, and posture shifts, among others.

When choosing non-verbal behaviours to accompany the speech of an embodied conversational agent (ECA), it is necessary to translate general findings from observing human behaviour into concrete selection strategies. There are two main implementation techniques that have been used for making this decision. In some systems, recorded behaviours are analysed and rules are created by hand based on the analysis; in others, recorded human data is used directly in the decision process. The former technique is similar to the classic role of corpora in natural-language generation described by Reiter and Dale (2000), while the latter is more similar to the more recent data-driven techniques that have been adopted (Belz and Varges, 2005).

Researchers that have used rule-based techniques to create embodied-agent systems include: Poggi and Pelachaud (2000), who concentrated on generating appropriate affective facial displays based on descriptions of typical facial expressions of emotion; Cassell et al. (2001a), who selected gestures and facial expressions to accompany text using heuristics derived from studies of typical North American non-verbal-displays; and Marsi and van Rooden (2007), who generated typical certain and uncertain facial displays for a talking head in an information-retrieval system. Researchers that used data-driven techniques include: Stone et al. (2004), who captured the motions of an actor performing scripted output and then used that data to create performance

Proceedings of the Workshop on Embodied Language Processing, pages 1–8,
Prague, Czech Republic, June 28, 2007.

specifications on the fly; Cassell et al. (2001b), who selected posture shifts for an embodied agent based on recorded human behaviour; and Kipp (2004), who annotated the gesturing behaviour of skilled public speakers and derived "gesture profiles" to use in the generation process.

Using rules derived from the data can produce displays that are easily identifiable and is straightforward to implement. On the other hand, making direct use of the data can produce output that is more similar to actual human behaviour by incorporating naturalistic variation, although it generally requires a more complex selection algorithm. In this paper, we investigate the relative utility of the two implementation strategies for a particular decision: selecting the conversational facial displays of an animated talking head. We use two methods for comparison: gathering users' subjective preferences, and measuring the impact of both selection strategies on users' ability to perceive user tailoring in speech.

In Section 2, we first describe how we recorded and annotated a corpus of facial displays in the domain of the target generation system. Section 3 then presents the two strategies that were implemented to select facial displays based on this corpus: one using a simple rule derived from the most characteristic behaviours in the corpus, and one that made a weighted choice among all of the options found in the corpus for each context. The next sections describe two user studies comparing these strategies: in Section 4, we compare users' subjective preferences, while in Section 5 we measure the impact of each strategy on user's ability to select spoken descriptions correctly tailored to a given set of user preferences. Finally, in Section 6, we discuss the results of these two studies, draw some conclusions, and outline potential future work.

2 Corpus collection and annotation[1]

The recording scripts for the corpus were created by the output planner of the COMIC multimodal dialogue system (Foster et al., 2005) and consisted of a total of 444 sentences describing and comparing various tile-design options. The surface form of each sentence was created by the OpenCCG surface realiser (White, 2006), using a grammar that specified both the words and the intended prosody for the speech synthesiser. We attached all of the relevant contextual, syntactic, and prosodic information to each node in the OpenCCG derivation tree, including the user-model evaluation of the object being described (positive, negative, or neutral), the predicted pitch accent, the clause of the sentence (first, second, or only), and whether the information being presented was new to the discourse.

The sentences in the script were presented one at a time to a speaker who was instructed to read each out loud as expressively as possible into a camera directed at his face. The following facial displays were then annotated on the recordings: eyebrow motions (up or down), eye squinting, and rigid head motion on all three axes (nodding, leaning, and turning). Each of these displays was attached to the node or nodes in the OpenCCG derivation tree that exactly covered the span of words temporally associated with the display. Two coders separately processed the sentences in the corpus. Using a version of the β weighted agreement measure proposed by Artstein and Poesio (2005)—which allows for a range of agreement levels the agreement on the sentences processed by both coders was 0.561.

When the distribution of facial displays in the corpus was analysed, it was found that the single biggest influence on the speaker's behaviour was the user-model evaluation of the features being described. When he described features of the design that had positive user-model evaluations, he was more likely to turn to the right and to raise his eyebrows (Figure 1(a)); on the other hand, on features with negative user-model evaluations, he was more likely to lean to the left, lower his eyebrows, and squint his eyes (Figure 1(b)). The overall most frequent display in all contexts was a downward nod on its own. Other factors that had a significant effect on the facial displays included the predicted pitch accent, the clause of the sentence (first or second), and the number of words spanned by a node.

3 Selection strategies

Based on the recorded behaviour of the speaker, we implemented two different methods for selecting facial displays to accompany synthesised speech. Both methods begin with the OpenCCG derivation

[1] Foster (2007) gives more details of the face-display corpus.

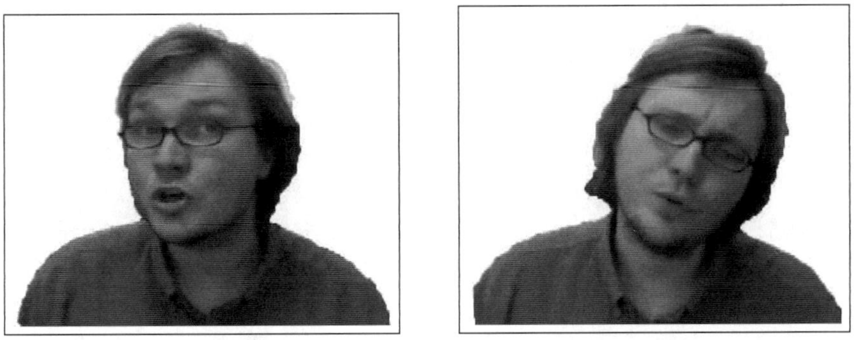

(a) Positive (b) Negative

Figure 1: Characteristic facial displays from the corpus

	Although	*it's*	*in*	*the*	*family*	*style,*	*the*	*tiles*	*are*	*by*	*Alessi.*
Original	nd=d	nd=d	nd=d		nd=d				nd=d,bw=u		
	.... ln=l										
Data-driven	nd=d				nd=d		.. tn=r ..				
Rule-based					ln=l,bw=d,sq						tn=r,bw=u

Figure 2: Face-display schedules for a sample sentence

tree for a sentence—that is, a tree in the same format as those that were used for the corpus annotation, including all of the contextual features. They then proceed top-down through the derivation tree, considering each node in turn and determining the display combination (if any) to accompany it.

The rule-based strategy specifies motions only on nodes corresponding to mentions of specific properties of a tile design: manufacturer and series names, colours, and decorations. The display combination is determined by the user-model evaluation of the property being described, based on the behaviours of the recorded speaker. For a positive evaluation, this strategy selects a right turn and brow raise; for a negative evaluation, it selects a left turn, brow lower, and eye squint; while for neutral evaluations, it chooses a downward nod.

In contrast, the data-driven strategy considers all nodes in the derivation tree. For each node, it selects from all of the display combinations that occurred on similar nodes in the corpus, weighted by the frequency. As a concrete example, in a hypothetical context where the speaker made no motion 80% of the time, nodded 15% of the time, and turned to the right in the other 5%, this strategy would select no motion with probability 0.8, a nod with probability 0.15, and a right turn with probability 0.05.

Figure 2 shows a sample sentence from the corpus, the original facial displays, and the displays selected by each of the strategies. In the figure, *nd=d* indicates a downward nod, *bw=u* and *bw=d* a brow raise and lower, respectively, *sq* an eye squint, *ln=l* a left lean, and *tn=r* a right turn.

4 Subjective preferences

As a first comparison of the two implementation strategies, we gathered users' subjective preferences between three different types of face-display schedules: the displays selected by each of the generation strategies described in the preceding section, as well as the original displays annotated in the corpus.

4.1 Participants

This experiment was run through the Language Experiments Portal,[2] a website dedicated to online psycholinguistic experiments. There were a total of 36 participants: 20 females and 16 males. 23 of the participants were between 20 and 29 years old, 9 were over 30, and 4 were under 20. 21 described themselves as expert computer users, 14 as intermediate users, and one as a beginner. 18 were native speakers of English, while the others had a range of other native languages.

[2] `http://www.language-experiments.org/`

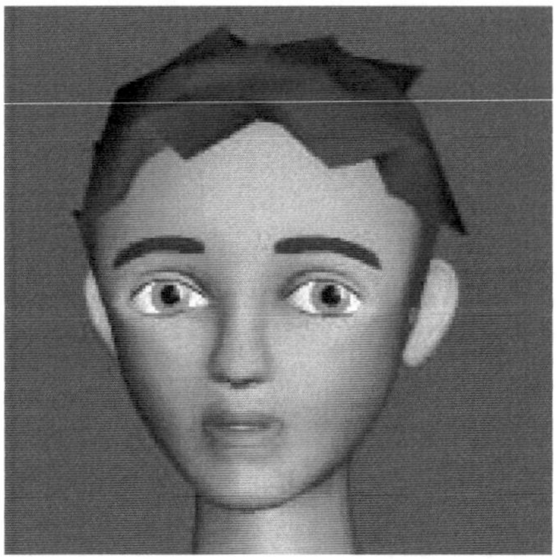

Figure 3: RUTH talking head

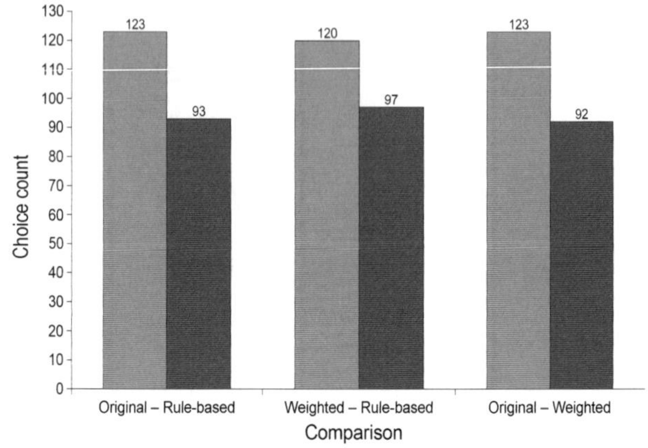

Figure 4: Subjective-preference results

4.2 Methodology

Each participant saw videos of two possible synthesised face-display schedules accompanying a series of 18 sentences. Both videos had the same synthesised speech, but each had a different different facial-display schedule. For each pair, the participant was asked to select which of the two versions they preferred. There were three different schedule types: the original displays annotated in the corpus, along with the output of both of the selection strategies. Participants made each pairwise comparison between these types six times, three times in each order. All participants saw the same set of sentences, in a random order: the pairwise choices were also allocated to sentences randomly.

4.3 Materials

To create the materials for this experiment, we randomly selected 18 sentences from the corpus and generated facial displays for each, using both of the strategies. The data-driven schedules were generated through 10-fold cross-validation as part of a previous study (Foster and Oberlander, 2007): that is, the display counts from 90% of the corpus were used to select the displays to use for the sentences in the held-out 10%. The rule-based schedules were generated by running the rule-based procedure from Section 3 on the same OpenCCG derivation trees. Videos were then created of all of the schedules for all of the sentences, using the Festival speech synthesiser (Clark et al., 2004) and the RUTH animated talking head (DeCarlo et al., 2004) (Figure 3).

4.4 Results

The overall results of this study are shown in Figure 4. Not all participants responded to all items, so there were a total of 648 responses: 216 comparing the original corpus schedules to the rule-based schedules, 217 for the data-driven vs. rule-based comparison, and 215 for the original vs. data-driven comparison. To assess the significance of the preferences, we use a binomial test, which provides an exact measure of the statistical significance of deviations from a theoretically expected classification into two categories. This test indicates that there was a mildly significant preference for the original schedules over the output of each of the strategies ($p < 0.05$ in both cases). While there was also a tendency to prefer the output of the data-driven strategy over that of the rule-based strategy, this preference was not significant ($p \approx 0.14$). No demographic factor had a significant effect on these results.

4.5 Discussion

Although there was no significant preference between the output of the two strategies, the generated schedules were very different. The rule-based strategy used only the three display combinations described in Section 3 and selected an average of 1.78 displays per sentence on the 18 sentences used in this study, while the data-driven strategy selected 12 different display combinations across the sentences and chose an average of 5.06 displays per sentence. For comparison, the original sentences from the corpus used a total of 15 different combinations on the

(1) Here is a family design. Its tiles are from the Lollipop collection by Agrob Buchtal. Although the tiles have a blue colour scheme, it does also feature green.

(2) Here is a family design. As you can see, the tiles have a blue and green colour scheme. It has floral motifs and artwork on the decorative tiles.

Figure 5: Tile-design description tailored to two user models (conflicting concession highlighted)

same sentences and had an average of 4.83 displays per sentence. In other words, in terms of the range of displays, the schedules generated by the data-driven strategy are fairly similar to those in the corpus, while those from the rule-based strategy do not resemble the corpus very much at all.

In another study (Foster and Oberlander, 2007), the weighted data-driven strategy used here was compared to a majority strategy that always chose the highest-probability option in every context. In other words, in the hypothetical context mentioned earlier where the top option occurred 80% of the time, the majority strategy would always choose that option. This strategy scored highly on an automated cross-validation study; however, human judges very strongly preferred the output of the weighted strategy described in this paper ($p < 0.0001$). This contrasts with the weak preference for the weighted strategy over the rule-based strategy in the current experiment. The main difference between the output of the majority strategy on the one hand, and that of the two strategies described here on the other, is in the distribution of the face-display combinations: over 90% of the that the majority strategy selected a display, it used a downward nod on its own, while both of the other strategies tended to generate a more even distribution of displays across the sentences. This suggests that the distribution of facial displays is more important than strict corpus similarity for determining subjective preferences.

The participants in this study generally preferred the original corpus displays to the output of either of the generation strategies. This suggests that a more sophisticated data-driven implementation that reproduces the corpus data more faithfully could be successful. For example, the process of selecting facial displays could be integrated directly into the OpenCCG realiser's n-gram-guided search for a good realisation (White, 2006), rather than being run on the output of the realiser as was done here.

5 Perception of user tailoring in speech

The results of the preceding experiment indicate that participants mildly preferred the output of the data-driven strategy to that of the rule-based strategy; however, this preference was not statistically significant. In this second experiment, we compare the face-display schedules generated by both strategies in a different way: measuring the impact of each schedule type on users' ability to detect user-model tailoring in synthesised speech.

Foster and White (2005) performed an experiment in which participants were shown a series of pairs of COMIC outputs (e.g., Figure 5) and asked to choose which was correctly tailored to a given set of user preferences. The participants in that study were able to select the correctly-tailored output only on trials where one option contained a concession to a negative preference that the other did not. For example, the description in (1) contains the concession *Although the tiles have a blue colour scheme*, as if the user disliked the colour blue, while (2) has no such concession. Figure 6 shows the results from that study when outputs were presented as speech; the results for text were nearly identical. The first pair of bars represent the choices made on trials where there was a conflicting concession, while the second pair show the choices made on trials with no conflicting concession. Using a binomial test, the difference for the conflicting-concession trials is significant at $p < 0.0001$, while there is no significant difference for the other trials ($p \approx 0.4$).

In this experiment, use the same experimental materials, but we use the talking head to present the system turns. This experiment allows us to answer two questions: whether the addition of a talking head affects users' ability to perceive tailoring in speech, and whether there is a difference between the impact of the two selection strategies.

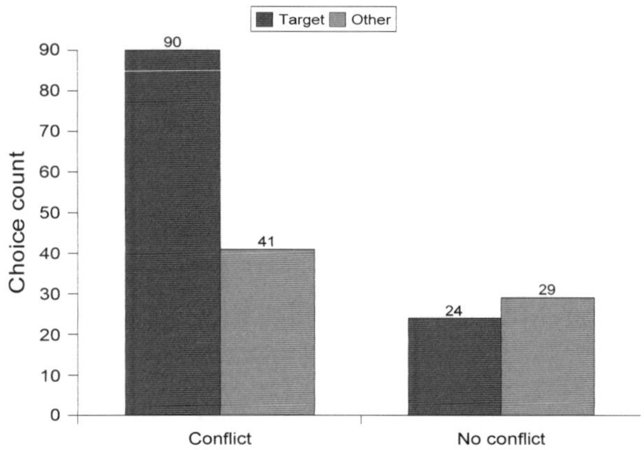

Figure 6: Results for speech-only presentation

5.1 Participants

Like the previous study, this one was also run over the web. There were 32 participants: 19 females and 13 males. 18 of the participants were between 20 and 29 years old, 10 were over 30, and 4 were under 20. 15 described themselves as expert computer users, 15 as intermediate users, and 2 as beginners. 30 of the participants were native English speakers.

5.2 Methodology

Participants in this experiment observed an eight-turn dialogue between the system and a user with specific likes and dislikes. The user preferences were displayed on screen at all times; the user input was presented as written text on the screen, while the system outputs were played as RUTH videos in response to the user clicking on a button. There were two versions of each system turn, one tailored to the preferences of the given user and one to the preferences of another user; the user task was to select the correctly tailored version. The order of presentation was counterbalanced so that the correctly tailored version was the first option in four of the trials and the second in the other four. Participants were assigned in rotation to one of four randomly-generated user models. As an additional factor, half of the participants saw videos with facial displays generated by the data-driven strategy, while the other half saw videos generated by the rule-based strategy.

5.3 Materials

The user models and dialogues were identical to those used by Foster and White (2005). For each sentence in each system turn, we annotated the nodes of the OpenCCG derivation tree with all of the necessary information for generation: the user-model evaluation, the pitch accents, the clause of the sentence, and the surface string. We then used those annotated trees to create face-display schedules using both of the selection strategies, using the full corpus as context for the data-driven strategy, and prepared RUTH videos of all of the generated schedules as in the previous study.

5.4 Results

The results of this study are shown in Figure 7: Figure 7(a) shows the results for the participants using the rule-based schedules, while Figure 7(b) shows the results with the data-driven schedules. Just as in the speech-only condition, the participants in this experiment responded essentially at chance on trials where there was no conflicting concession to negative preferences. For the trials with a conflicting concession, participants using rule-based videos selected the targeted version significantly more often ($p < 0.01$), while the results for participants using the data-driven videos show no significant trend ($p \approx 0.49$). None of the demographic factors affected these results.

To assess the significance of the difference between the two selection strategies, we compared the results on the conflicting-concession trials from each of the groups to the corresponding results from the speech-only experiment, using a χ^2 test. The results for the judges using the rule-based videos are very similar to those of the judges using only speech ($\chi^2 = 0.21$, $p = 0.65$). However, there is a significant difference between the responses of the speech-only judges and those of the judges using the weighted schedules ($\chi^2 = 4.72$, $p < 0.05$).

5.5 Discussion

The materials for this study were identical to those used by Foster and White (2005); in fact, the waveforms for the synthesised speech were identical. However, the participants in this study who saw the videos generated by the data-driven strategy

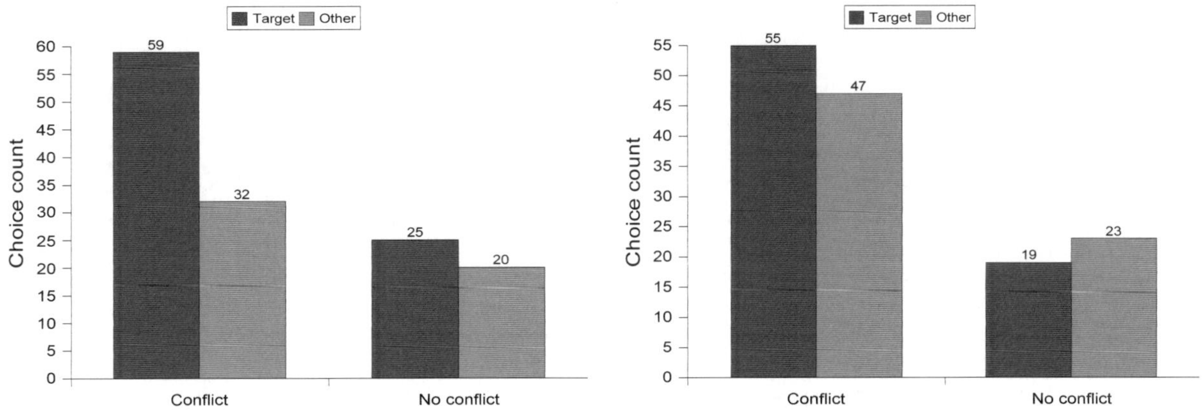

(a) Rule-based schedules

(b) Data-driven schedules

Figure 7: Results of the perception study

were significantly worse at identifying the correctly-tailored speech than were the participants in the previous study, while the performance of the participants who saw rule-based videos was essentially identical to that of the speech-only subjects.

The schedules selected by the data-driven strategy for this evaluation include a variety of facial displays; sometimes these displays are actually the opposite of what would be selected by the rule-based strategy. For example, the head moves to the right when describing a negative fact in 23 of the 520 data-driven schedules, and moves to the left when describing a neutral or positive fact in 20 cases. A description includes up to three sentences, and a trial involved comparing two descriptions, so a total of 75 of the trials (52%) for the data-driven participants involved at least one of these these potentially misleading head movements. Across all of the trials for the participants using data-driven videos, there were 38 conflicting-concession trials with no such head movement. The performance on these trials was essentially the identical to that on the full set of trials: the correctly targeted description was chosen 20 times, and the other version 18 times. So the worse performance with the data-driven schedules cannot be attributed solely to the selected facial displays conflicting with the linguistic content.

Another possibility is that the study participants who used the data-driven schedules were distracted by the expressive motions of the talking head and failed to pay attention to the content of the speech. This appears to have been the case in the COMIC whole-system evaluation (White et al., 2005), for example, where the performance of the male participants on a recall task was significantly worse when a more expressive talking head was used. On this study, there was no effect of gender (or any of the other demographic factors) on the pattern of responses; however, it could be that a similar effect occurred in this study for all of the participants.

6 Conclusions and future work

The experiments in this paper have compared the two main current implementation techniques for choosing non-verbal behaviour for an embodied conversational agent: using rules derived from the study of human behaviour, and using recorded human behaviour directly in the generation process. The results of the subjective-preference evaluation indicate that participants tended to prefer the output generated by the data-driven strategy, although this preference was not significant. In the second study, videos generated by the data-driven strategy significantly decreased participants' ability to detect correctly-tailored spoken output when compared to a speech-only presentation; on the other hand, videos generated by the rule-based strategy did not have a significant impact on this task.

These results indicate that, at least for this corpus and this generation task, the choice of generation strategy depends largely on which aspect of the system is more important: to create an agent that users like subjectively, or to ensure that users fully understand all aspects of the output presented in speech. If the former is more important, than an implementation that uses the data directly appears to be a slightly better option; if the latter is more important, then the rule-based strategy seems superior.

On the subjective-preference evaluation, users preferred the original corpus motions over either of the generated versions. As discussed in Section 4.5, this suggests that there is room for a more sophisticated data-driven selection strategy that reproduces the corpus data more closely. The output of such a generation strategy might also have a different effect on the perception task.

Both of these studies used the RUTH talking head (Figure 3), which has no body and, while human in appearance, is not particularly realistic. We used this head to investigate the the generation of a limited set of facial displays, based on contextual information including the user-model evaluation, the predicted prosody, the clause of the sentence, and the surface string. More information about the relative utility of different techniques for selecting non-verbal behaviour for embodied agents can be gathered by experimenting with a wider range of agents and of non-verbal behaviours. Other possible agent types include photorealistic animated agents, agents with fully articulated virtual bodies, and physically embodied robot agents. The possibilities for non-verbal behaviours include deictic, iconic, and beat gestures, body posture, gaze behaviour, and facial expressions of various types of affect, while any source of syntactic or pragmatic context could be used to help make the selection. Experimenting with other combinations of agent properties and behaviours can improve our knowledge of the relative utility of different mechanisms for selecting non-verbal behaviour.

References

R. Artstein and M. Poesio. 2005. Kappa^3 = alpha (or beta). Technical Report CSM-437, University of Essex Department of Computer Science.

J. B. Bavelas and N. Chovil. 2000. Visible acts of meaning: An integrated message model of language in face-to-face dialogue. *Journal of Language and Social Psychology*, 19(2):163–194. doi:10.1177/0261927X00019002001.

A. Belz and S. Varges, editors. 2005. *Corpus Linguistics 2005 Workshop on Using Corpora for Natural Language Generation*. http://www.itri.brighton.ac.uk/ucnlg/ucnlg05/.

T. Bickmore and J. Cassell. 2005. Social dialogue with embodied conversational agents. In J. van Kuppevelt, L. Dybkjær, and N. Bernsen, editors, *Advances in Natural, Multimodal Dialogue Systems*. Kluwer, New York. doi:10.1007/1-4020-3933-6_2.

J. Cassell, T. Bickmore, H. Vilhjálmsson, and H. Yan. 2001a. More than just a pretty face: Conversational protocols and the affordances of embodiment. *Knowledge-Based Systems*, 14(1–2):55–64. doi:10.1016/S0950-7051(00)00102-7.

J. Cassell, Y. Nakano, T. W. Bickmore, C. L. Sidner, and C. Rich. 2001b. Non-verbal cues for discourse structure. In *Proceedings of the 39th Annual Meeting of the Association for Computational Linguistics (ACL 2001)*. ACL Anthology P01-1016.

R. A. J. Clark, K. Richmond, and S. King. 2004. Festival 2 – build your own general purpose unit selection speech synthesiser. In *Proceedings of the 5th ISCA Workshop on Speech Synthesis*.

D. DeCarlo, M. Stone, C. Revilla, and J. Venditti. 2004. Specifying and animating facial signals for discourse in embodied conversational agents. *Computer Animation and Virtual Worlds*, 15(1):27–38. doi:10.1002/cav.5.

M. E. Foster. 2007. Associating facial displays with syntactic constituents for generation. In *Proceedings of the ACL 2007 Workshop on Linguistic Annotation (The LAW)*.

M. E. Foster and J. Oberlander. 2007. Corpus-based generation of conversational facial displays. In submission.

M. E. Foster and M. White. 2005. Assessing the impact of adaptive generation in the COMIC multimodal dialogue system. In *Proceedings of the IJCAI 2005 Workshop on Knowledge and Reasoning in Practical Dialogue Systems*.

M. E. Foster, M. White, A. Setzer, and R. Catizone. 2005. Multimodal generation in the COMIC dialogue system. In *Proceedings of the ACL 2005 Demo Session*. ACL Anthology W06-1403.

M. Kipp. 2004. *Gesture Generation by Imitation - From Human Behavior to Computer Character Animation*. Dissertation.com.

E. Marsi and F. van Rooden. 2007. Expressing uncertainty with a talking head. In *Proceedings of the Workshop on Multimodal Output Generation (MOG 2007)*.

I. Poggi and C. Pelachaud. 2000. Performative facial expressions in animated faces. In J. Cassell, J. Sullivan, S. Prevost, and E. Churchill, editors, *Embodied Conversational Agents*, pages 154–188. MIT Press.

E. Reiter and R. Dale. 2000. *Building Natural Language Generation Systems*. Cambridge University Press. doi:10.2277/052102451X.

M. Stone, D. DeCarlo, I. Oh, C. Rodriguez, A. Lees, A. Stere, and C. Bregler. 2004. Speaking with hands: Creating animated conversational characters from recordings of human performance. *ACM Transactions on Graphics (TOG)*, 23(3):506–513. doi:10.1145/1015706.1015753.

M. White. 2006. Efficient realization of coordinate structures in Combinatory Categorial Grammar. *Research on Language and Computation*, 4(1):39–75. doi:10.1007/s11168-006-9010-2.

M. White, M. E. Foster, J. Oberlander, and A. Brown. 2005. Using facial feedback to enhance turn-taking in a multimodal dialogue system. In *Proceedings of HCI International 2005*.

Aiduti in Japanese Multi-party Design Conversations

Yasuhiro Katagiri
Future University - Hakodate
116-2 Kameda-Nakano Hakodate Hokkaido, Japan
katagiri@fun.ac.jp

Abstract

Japanese backchannel utterances, aizuti, in a multi-party design conversation were examined, and aizuti functions were analyzed in comparison with its functions in two-party dialogues. In addition to the two major functions, signaling acknowledgment and turn-management, it was argued that aizuti in multi-party conversations are involved in joint construction of design plans through management of the floor structure, and display of participants' readiness to engage in collaborative elaboration of jointly constructed proposals.

1 Introduction

Backchannel utterances are one of the representative phenomena characterizing conversational interactions. We can find backchannel utterances in every natural conversation in every culture. Different languages have different repertoire of expressions that work as backchannels. In terms of what functions they serve in conversations, it has widely been acknowledged that backchannels, by conveying the hearer feedback to the speaker, serve to contribute to informational coordination between conversational participants, through conversational flow management in terms of both common grounding and smooth turn-taking. It has also been acknowledged, perhaps less explicitly, that backchannels serve to contribute to affective coordination by promoting rapport between conversational participants. It is still unclear how these two contrasting views on backchannels can be integrated. How are the informational and the affective coordination functions of backchannels inter-related? What factors determine relative salience of these two functions in certain usage of backchannels? Are there any categories of conversational interactions that promote one or the other functions? Are there cultural differences in backchannel usages?

We focus, in this paper, on the use of Japanese backchannels, aiduti, in multi-party conversations. Based on the analysis of how aiduti utterances are employed in experimentally captured multi-party design conversation data, we argue that aiduti utterances in Japanese have, on top of the informational coordination functions of common-grounding and turn-management, the function of expressing the readiness, a positive attitude, on the part of a participant to engage in the joint construction of an ongoing proposal currently under discussion, which then leads to affective coordination.

2 Backchannels in Dialogues

Backchannel utterances were conceived initially in two-party dialogues with one speaker and one hearer. Schegloff (1982) picked up hearer's short utterances such as 'uh, huh' produced in response to the speaker's main utterances, and characterized them as backchannels, whose functions are to convey backward messages from the hearer to the speaker indicating that the hearer is attending to, listening to, understanding, and expecting to continue the production of the speaker's main message.

Heritage (2006) provides a broader conception of backchannels and lists the following four functions

Proceedings of the Workshop on Embodied Language Processing, pages 9–16,
Prague, Czech Republic, June 28, 2007.

Figure 1: Meeting archiver equipment MARC used in data collection

Figure 2: Setting for multi-party design conversation capture

for backchannel utterances.

- Provide Acknowledgments to prior locutions by the speaker
- Projection of further talk in turn taking
- Recipient epistemic states triggered by the speaker's message
- Recipient affiliative attitude, how the recipient is aligned with speaker's message

Maynard (1986) compared Japanese and American dialogues, and observed that Japanese dialogues have almost twice as much aizuti as American backchannel utterances. This observation suggests that significance of backchannels and their functions in conversational interactions may depend on social groups, types of activities and other social or task related parameters.

3 Multi-party Conversation

3.1 Varieties of multi-party conversations

We will focus on aiduti utterances in Japanese multi-party design conversations. In order to locate the type of activity we've been working on within the broad range of interaction activities collectively categorized as multi-party conversations, we first try to list up potential parameters that might influence the structure and organization of conversational interactions.

Number of participants

We call a conversation between more than two people a multi-party conversation. A conversation between three people and a conversation between 10 people are not the same in their conversational organization. It has been observed (Fay et al., 2000) that conversations with a small number of participants tend to be homogeneous that contain a number of equal status pairwise interactions, whereas conversations with a large number of participants tend to be more hierarchical with a central control person working as a chairperson.

Types of activities

Conversational interactions are often embedded in larger activities, and the type of embedding activities makes a difference in the organization of conversations.

(a) Purpose
One-way information transfer in lectures and joint problem solving in a group of people have both fixed but different types of goals. When people chat for socialization, having a conversation itself becomes its own purpose. These different types of goals could produce different organizational structures in conversations.

(b) Rigidity of purpose
Even within joint problem solving activities,

Sp	Utterance
D:	普段
D:	その携帯会社変えないにしても使ってて
D:	メールアドレスが:そのもう１個持てたら
	(I often think that even when you keep using the same mobile carrier, if you could have one more mail address,)
E:	うんうんうん **(un-un-un)**
D:	いいなあとか
	(it would be nice)
D:	パソコンだったらいくらでも
	(with PC, any number of addresses)
F:	うんうん **(un-un)**
E:	ああ:あはいはいはいはい **(aa-aa, hai-hai-hai-hai)**
D:	持てるじゃないですか
	(you can have)
F:	(D_ノー)
B:	うん **(un)**:
C:	うん **(un)**
D:	あそういうのは
E:	うん **(un)**
D:	欲しいなと思いますよ
	(I would definitely want one)
B:	うん **(un)**:
E:	(D_ンドー)
E:	メルアドを複数ってことですよね
	(You mean, multiple mail addresses, right?)
D:	はい **(hai)**
C:	うん **(un)**:
C:	まあお年寄り向けの
	(for elderly people)
E:	うんうん **(un-un)**
C:	あの:
B:	うん **(un)**
C:	ていうかお年寄りというか (D_バ) 僕の親
C:	(laugh)
C:	なぞとですねメールをやり取りしようとすると
	(when I try to correspond by mail with elderly, eh, with my parents)
E:	うんうん **(un-un)**
B:	うん **(un)**
E:	うん **(un)**
C:	まあ親は:打てないんです:よね
	(parents cannot type)
B:	うん **(un)**
E:	うん **(un)**
C:	でも通話はできる
	(but, they can talk on the phone)
B:	うん **(un)**
E:	うんうん **(un-un)**
C:	でもあの:やり取りできればメールでやりたいと
	(but, when you'd rather want to use mails, if possible)
E:	うんうんうん **(un-un-un)**
B:	うん **(un)**
C:	いう場合
F:	うん **(un)**
C:	例えば:
C:	音声認識で:
	(how about, with speech recognition)
E:	ああ **(aa)** いいですね:
	(that's good)
B:	うん **(un)**:
C:	文章んなっ
	(convert speech into text)

Figure 3: Aiduti in design conversation

we can conceive of different degree of rigidity of problem goals conversational participants are working on. In one extreme lies a pursuit of a fixed goal such as mathematical problem solving, in which a problem with a clearly determined answer is given to the group. In other extreme lies a problem solving under a loosely stated goal such as floor planning of an apartment for the group, in which the only requirement is to reach an agreement, and factors to consider must be made explicit in the course of conversation. The design conversation we've looked at belong to the latter category.

(c) Reality
Every experimental data collection has to face this problem. Whether or not and how much the outcome of the conversation has real import in participants' life makes a big difference in conversational organization.

(d) Use of objects
Use of physical objects, particularly informational artifact such as whiteboard and projectors, changes the use pattern of multi-modal signals: gaze, gestures and body postures, and needs to be taken into account in experimental data collection.

Characteristics of participants

(a) Participant properties
Differences in capabilities such as in knowledge and in expertise, and dispositional properties, such as preferences, beliefs, and personalities of participants greatly contribute to shape the interaction.

(b) Participant roles

Start -End	Sp	Utterances
243.1950-243.7450	F:	are-wo
-		(that)
244.2075-246.1200	F:	tatoeba keitai-wo nakusita toki-no sono
-		(when you lose your mobile phone)
246.6300-247.9800	F:	timei-tekina doai-wa
-		(how fatal it will be)
248.2725-248.8850	F:	nn daibu
-		(big)
248.7550-249.7350	B:	**un:**
249.3000-250.0200	E:	**un:**
249.5150-249.8225	D:	**un:**
250.1250-254.8225	F:	**un:**are ikko otosityattara ironna houmen-no raihu-rain-ga soredakede tataretyautte iunoga atte
-		(if you lose one, your life line will be cut out in a lot of ways)

Figure 4: Aiduti overlap

Conversation setting often dictates certain role assignment to each participant, which in turn determines the shape of interactions that takes place between people under those participant roles. Instructor and follower in instruction giving tasks, and clerk and customer in commercial transactions are typical examples. The role of chairperson also is significant in determining the structure of conversations.

(c) Participant relationships
Age and social status often provide a fixed base for dominance relationship among conversational participants. Affiliative familiarity between participants are less fixed but still stable relationships. Sharing of opinions is temporary and can change quite quickly during the course of a conversation.

3.2 Multi-party design conversation

We have been collecting data on multi-party design conversation in Japanese. Multi-party design conversation is a type of joint problem solving conversation, in which participants engage in a discussion to come up with an agreement on the final design plan. The design goal, however, is only partially specified, and participants need to jointly decide on evaluative criteria for the design goal during the course of the discussion.

Start -End	Sp	Utterance
781.5050-781.6100	C:	あ
781.7750-782.7050	C:	じゃもう１つちょっとあの
-		(one more thing)
782.6300-782.8900	E:	はい
782.9550-784.4925	C:	あのコミニケーション関係で
-		(related to communication)
784.6050-784.7750	E:	うん
784.6500-786.6450	C:	ちょっとだけあの思いつきなんですけど:
-		(just a thought)
786.1925-786.6950	E:	うんうん
787.3475-788.4875	C:	あの:まメールとか:
788.6125-789.9975	C:	あのやり取りするときとか:
790.5375-790.6175	C:	(W_ト—特に)
790.7975-792.2575	C:	特にま携帯メールとかだと:
792.6125-795.7250	C:	ま結構あのパソコンメールと違って早めの返事を
-		(when you exchange mails, particularly on mobile phones, people expect quicker responses)
		...
830.4175-831.7750	C:	まそんなようなのがわかると
831.7125-832.0400	B:	え:
832.1475-833.1475	E:	あ:
832.3675-833.3750	C:	まいいかな:みたいな
832.3875-834.4525	B:	ドライブモードのなんか
-		(drive mode)
834.4450-835.5700	E:	あ:ん
834.6325-834.9900	C:	ええ
834.8000-836.3450	B:	携帯版みたいな感じで
-		(on the mobile phone)
836.0075-837.5475	C:	ええああドライブモードってある
-		(Ah, I know drive mode)
837.4525-842.8250	B:	(W_エント—えーと) なんかこう今運転中ですみたいなのがこう電話すると出るのと同じで
-		(same as, when you make a call, it says it's on drive now)
-		...
844.8375-846.2475	B:	そういうのが返ってくる
-		(you get those responses)
845.1450-846.6375	E:	結構簡単にできそうですよね
-		(it seems rather simple to realize)
846.2325-846.3950	C:	うん
846.5650-846.7850	C:	うん
846.5750-848.2600	D:	あのヤフーメッセンジャーってあるじゃないですか
-		(you know Yahoo messenger?)
847.5825-847.8575	B:	咳
847.9050-848.5125	E:	うん:
848.1400-848.6200	B:	うん:
848.4450-849.5650	D:	あれ使ってると:その
849.9125-851.3250	D:	メッセンジャーの相手の状況が
-		(you can see the situation of your correspondent)
851.3600-851.8900	E:	うん:

Figure 5: Floor structure

Speaker	Utterance	Aiduti
A	158	3
B	426	179
C	420	125
D	346	138
E	612	343
F	206	69
Total	2,168	857

Table 1: Number of utterances and aiduti produced in multi-party design conversation

Japanese form	sound	translation
はい	hai	(yes)
うん	un	(yeah)
ああ	aa	(ah)
ええ	ee	(correct)
そう	sou	(I agree)

Table 2: Linguistic forms of aiduti

The condition of our data collection was as follows:

Number of participants: six for each session

Arrangement: face-to-face conversation

Task: Proposal for a new mobile phone business

Role: No pre-determined role was imposed

In order to minimize the intimidating effect of a huge recording setup, we used a compact meeting archiver equipment, MARC, currently under development in AIST Japan (Asano and Ogata, 2006) shown in Fig. 1. MARC is equipped with an array of 6 cameras together with an array of 8 microphones, and it captures panoramic video with up to 15 frames/sec. and speaker-separated speech streams with 16kHz sampling rate. A meeting capture scene is shown in Fig. 2.

The data we examine in this paper consists of one 30 minutes conversation conducted by 5 males and 1 female. Even though we did not assign any roles, a chairperson and a clerk were spontaneously elected by the participants at the beginning of the session.

4 Aizuti in multi-party design conversation

4.1 Aiduti types and amounts

We first looked at how frequent people produce aiduti in the conversation. Table 1 shows the number of utterances and aiduti utterances for each of the six speakers, both in terms of the number of inter-pausal units (IPUs). Table 2 indicates expressions identified as aiduti utterances. Positive responses to questions and requests are not included in aiduti, even if they share the surface forms of Table 2. Reduplicated forms of each of the aiduti expressions in Table 2 are also frequently observed, and they were counted as one aiduti occurences.

We can see that a sizable portion of utterances, about 30% to 40%, were actually aiduti utterances in our data. An example excerpt demonstrating the abundance of aiduti is shown in Fig. 3, where aiduti utterances are marked by bold characters.

4.2 Conversation flow management

Overlapping aiduti

One reason why multi-party conversation contains a lot of aiduti is that there are more hearers, potential backchannel producers. Fig. 4 shows an example in which three hearers B,E, and D produced aiduti almost simultaneously to the speaker F's utterance. The fact that these three aiduti were overlapping shows that they are independently directed to the speaker F's preceding utterance. This type of aiduti response is expected to increase in numbers as the number of conversation participants increases.

Aiduti for turn-holding

In the same example in Fig. 4, the speaker F produced aiduti 'un' after all aiduti utterances by hearers B, E, and D, and immediately before he continued his turn. This type of speaker aiduti can be taken to serve the turn-holding function. It gives an acknowledgment to all the acknowledgments from hearers collectively and signals that the speaker is going on producing his own message.

Aiduti for floor transition

A relatively clear structure was observed in the conversation we analyzed. The conversation consisted of a sequence of idea proposals produced by

Aiduti→Floor	Num
Aiduti speaker becomes the next floor main speaker	53
non-Aiduti speaker becomes next floor main speaker	17
Total	70

Table 3: Aiduti and floor transition

different speakers. We identified a stretch of conversation as a floor in which one main speaker makes a proposal on his or her ideas. As long as the specific proposal is being discussed as the conversation topic, other participants may contribute clarification or elaboration utterances within the same floor. An example of a sequence of floors is shown in Fig. 5. C first talks about the difference in people's expected response between mobile mails and PC mails in the first floor. B then brings about in the second floor a suggestion on some functionality similar to drive mode which indicates to the original sender that the recipient is not available at the moment. D in the third floor follows on by mentioning Yahoo messenger. We extracted 71 floors total from the 30 minute conversation data.

Table 3 indicates the relationship between the production of aiduti in one floor and the claiming of the main speaker-hood in the next floor. The table shows that many of the main speaker of a floor had produced aiduti as a non-main speaker in the preceding floor. This suggests that aiduti utterances from non-main speakers indicate their readiness to make a positive contribution to the joint task, by taking the next floor and by contributing a proposal for the task when they find a suitable opportunity.

4.3 Collaborative elaboration of proposals

When we take a closer look into floors, we find positive collaborative behaviors from non-main speaker participants. Typical behaviors of non-main speaker participants of a floor include giving aiduti, providing (positive) evaluations to the idea proposed, and inserting clarification questions. On top of these behaviors, it was often observed in a floor that non-main speaker participants try to make positive contributions to the idea currently on the table, by adding new elements of ideas or providing concrete ideas to part of the proposal that heretofore remained vague at the time. We call these behaviors on the

Start -End	Sp	Utterance
505.2500-506.4500	D:	イメージとしてはその
-		(as an image)
505.4375-505.7225	E:	でも
506.8000-508.1450	D:	(W_サ—３) ３年後って書いてありますけどその
-		(this says three years from now)
508.6675-509.3500	D:	ＰＣと
509.4875-509.9375	E:	うん
509.5300-510.1400	D:	スカイプ
510.3875-510.9250	E:	うんうん
510.4875-511.1200	B:	あ:
510.5100-510.6650	D:	が
510.9125-511.5975	D:	くっついたような
511.8375-512.2125	E:	うん
512.0075-512.1975	B:	はい
512.1125-512.8725	D:	感じだとすごい
512.2650-512.8800	C:	あ:
512.6075-513.2850	B:	あ:
513.0050-514.0925	D:	便利だな:と思うんですけどね
-		(it would be really convenient to combine PC with Skype)
513.3875-514.2525	E:	うん
513.6325-514.1650	C:	いいですね
-		(good)
514.3150-515.2350	C:	スカイプ:で
-		(with Skype)
514.3725-515.5525	E:	うん
514.5375-515.3200	B:	いいっすね:
-		(good)
515.8950-516.0875	C:	やり
516.2775-516.4825	C:	ただ
516.8400-517.8825	C:	ただ通話し放題
-		(you can call free)
517.8100-518.8125	B:	ただ **(W_通—通話)**
-		(free call)
518.2200-520.8650	D:	ただ通話しまそのまあ電波の問題とかも解消して
-		(frequency assignment problem will somehow be solved)
518.2500-519.0475	C:	笑
519.0500-519.9925	B:	笑
519.5150-520.6675	C:	笑
520.4400-521.6825	E:	うんうんうんうんうん
520.6800-521.3675	B:	笑
521.5100-522.3050	B:	うん
521.8250-522.7875	E:	うん
521.9025-522.9375	D:	国際的に使えれば
-		(if its available worldwide)
522.7975-523.0550	C:	ええ

Figure 6: Collaborative elaboration: Success

Start -End	Sp	Utterance
543.1750-544.3800	C:	まあ今今:のなんか
544.6725-548.2050	C:	ま (W_グ—Ｇｏｏｇｌｅ)(W_グ—Ｇｏｏｇｌｅ) Ｇｏｏｇｌｅが (D_グ) やっているようなサービス:にもちょっと近いんですけど:
-		(this is closer to Google service)
546.8350-547.5825	E:	うん
548.5725-551.8350	C:	データーを端末じゃなくって:ネットワーク側の方に置いとけば:
-		(if we place data in the network rather than on the terminal)
551.4175-552.3400	E:	うん
551.7175-552.1175	B:	うん
552.4425-556.9450	C:	端末落っことしても:ま先ほど:のような形で使えないアクセスできないようにしておけば:
-		(even when we lose your terminal, if you setup so that other people can not use, not access)
553.7150-554.2625	E:	うんうん
554.3650-554.6675	D:	うん
556.2425-557.2450	E:	うんうん
556.7250-557.1150	B:	うん
557.5875-558.4275	C:	そっから見れない
-		(nobody can get data from there)
		...
567.2850-567.7400	B:	あ:
567.6250-567.9725	E:	うん
568.0075-568.8775	B:	バックアップが
569.0300-569.7200	B:	あったりとか
-		(there might be backup)
569.7725-570.4025	E:	うん
570.1050-570.7775	C:	ええま (W_バツ—バックアップ)
-		(well, backup)
570.2625-570.6350	D:	うん
571.1225-572.4825	B:	バックアップってことでもないか
-		(maybe backup is not such a good idea)
571.3425-573.5925	C:	バックアップだと端末:にデータが残っちゃうんで:
-		(backup leaves data on the terminal)
572.6925-573.2025	B:	そうか
-		(right)

Figure 7: Collaborative elaboration: failure

Condition	Num
Floor with aiduti	67
Floor with no aiduti	4
Floor with Collab-Elab.	29
Floor with no Collab-Elab.	42
Aiduti speaker initiated Collab-Elab.	25
non-Aiduti speaker initiated Collab-Elab.	4

Table 4: Aiduti in Collaborative elaboration

part of non-main speaker participants 'collaborative elaboration.' Collaborative elaboration can be a success or a failure. Figures 6 and 7 show two contrasting examples. In the example in Fig. 6, non-main speaker participants C and B successfully contribute to the idea proposal by the main speaker D on combining PC and Skype functionalities, by explicitly pointing out the concrete merit, e.g., free phone call, as a support of the proposal. In the example in Fig. 7, on the other hand, a non-main speaker participant B first tried to make a contribution, the idea of local data backup, to the proposal produced by the main speaker C, storage of data in the network, but gave up after a non-positive response from C and retracted his additional proposal.

Table 4 shows the relationship between collaborative evaluation and aiduti utterances in a floor. Aiduti utterances were observed in almost every floor. Collaborative elaboration is also rather frequent. It takes place in about 40% of all floors. Finally, the table shows that participants who perform collaborative evaluation in a floor are likely to produce aiduti utterances in the same floor. This suggests, again, that aiduti utterances from non-main speaker participants of a floor indicate their readiness to make a positive contribution to the joint task, by improving on the proposal currently being discussed.

5 Discussions

Frequency of aiduti utterances

We observed that multi-party conversations contain a high rate (30∼40%) of aiduti utterances. a great number of aiduti utterances were produced by the chairperson among all the participants. Saft (2006), based on the analysis of Japanese TV discussion programs, pointed out that chairperson produces a large portion of aiduti among all the discussion participants. These findings appear to confirm the idea that aiduti utterances have functions to manage the flow of conversations, and chairpersons exploit these functions in discussion sessions. But, exact conversation flow management function of aiduti may not be unique. According to Saft (2006), the chairperson in the particular TV discussion program uses aiduti to claim their addressee-hood in order to prevent the discussion from free-floating and out of control. In our design conversation data, it appears that the chairperson frequently inserts aiduti in order to encourage other participants to engage in the discussion and to make the session more lively.

Floor structure

It may not always be a good strategy for everybody to produce aiduti as acknowledgment in a multi-party conversation, since with a lot of hearers it can be a nuisance for the speaker to get too many aiduti in every possible grounding point. It follows that the fact that a certain participant produces aiduti at a certain timing in a multi-party conversation can have significance other than the grounding of the message just produced. It is interesting to note that even though at the level of turn-taking, an aiduti utterance works as a continuer, a turn-yielding signal, at the level of floor, aiduti utterances seem to indicate positive involvement attitude of the participant toward the joint problem solving activity.

Collaborative elaboration

We observed a number of instances of joint construction of proposals through collaborative elaboration in our design conversation data. It was also observed that in most of the cases of collaborative elaboration, aiduti utterances were accompanied by participants engaging in collaborative elaboration. These facts seem to imply that aiduti utterances both signal and produce among conversation participants an affiliative awareness toward joint construction of the proposal for the problem at hand, through the exchange of readiness signal, among all the group members, toward making positive contributions to the ongoing joint problem solving activity. We believe that these contribution readiness and affiliative awareness are the basis of affective functions of aiduti in Japanese conversations.

6 Conclusions

An analysis of aiduti utterances, Japanese backchannels, in a Japanese multi-party design conversation was conducted. It was argued, based on the analysis, that, in addition to the two major functions, signaling acknowledgment and turn-management, aiduti utterances in multi-party conversations are involved in joint construction of design plans through management of the floor structure, and display of participants' readiness to engage in collaborative elaboration of jointly constructed proposals. It was also suggested that these additional functions eventually lead to affective functions of aiduti.

Acknowledgment

The work reported in this paper was partially supported by Japan Society for the Promotion of Science Grants-in-aid for Scientific Research (B) 18300052.

References

Futoshi Asano and Jun Ogata. 2006. Detection and separation of speech events in meeting recordings. In *Proc. Interspeech*, pages 2586–2589.

Nicholas Fay, Simon Garrod, and Jean Carletta. 2000. Group discussion as interactive dialogue or as serial monologue: The influence of group size. *Psychological Science*, 11(6):487–492.

John Heritage. 2006. An overview of English backchannels. International workshop on cross-cultural and culture-specific aspects of conversational backchannels and feedback, December.

Senko K. Maynard. 1986. On back-channel behavior in Japanese and English casual conversation. *Linguistics*, 24:1079–1108.

Scott L. Saft. 2006. The moderator in control: Use of names, the particle ne, and response tokens on a Japanese discussion TV program. *Research on Language and Social Interaction*, 39(2):155–193.

Emanuel A. Schegloff. 1982. Discourse as interactional achievement: some uses of" uh huh" and other things that come between sentences. In Deborah Tannen, editor, *Analyzing Discourse, Text, and Talk*, pages 71–93. Georgetown University Press.

Computing Backchannel Distributions in Multi-Party Conversations

Dirk Heylen
Human Media Interaction
University of Twente
heylen@cs.utwente.nl

Rieks op den Akker
Human Media Interaction
University of Twente
infrieks@cs.utwente.nl

Abstract

In multi-party conversations it may not always be obvious who is talking to whom. Backchannels may provide a partial answer to this question, possibly in combination with some other events, such as gaze behaviors of the interlocutors. We look at some patterns in multi-party interaction relating features of backchannel behaviours to aspects of the partipation framework.

1 Introduction

In this paper we present a summary of our investigations into the distribution of back-channels and some other forms of feedback and assesments in argumentative multi-party discourse. We are interested in such expressions for several reasons. First, the sheer utterance of a backchannel indicates the presence of an auditor that indicates "I am here, I am attending". The fact that it is being uttered by an auditor indicates intrinsically that the auditor *felt addressed in some way or another* by the speaker. For the analysis of multi-party conversations, it is important to establish *who is talking to whom* and backchannels, at least seem to give away the *whom* part. Second, the exact form, the kind of vocalisation, the intonation and the context may further invest the utterance with additional meanings, expressing various attitudes towards what has been said: skepticism, surprise, liking, agreement, and so on. So, when we look at back-channels in the context of multi-party dialogues they may tell us something about the participation framework on the one hand (who was talking to whom) and about the way utterances are being assessed by their audience.

The qualifier "in some way or another" with respect to feeling or being addressed is particularly important in the context of multi-party dialogues (i.e. dialogues with more than two persons present). Typically, an utterance by a speaker instantiates the performance of a speech act with a particular illocutionary and perlocutionary force. The speech act involves a request for uptake. However, as has been pointed out several times (Goffman (Goffman, 1981), Levinson (Levinson, 1988), Clark and Carlson (Clark and Carlson, 1992), Schegloff (Schegloff, 1988)), participants in a multi-party conversation can have a different role or status and they can be addressed in different ways.

In this paper we report on some of our investigations into the distribution of backchannels in multiparty interactions (for instance in relation to other phenomena such as gaze) and how this information can help us to uncover certain features of floor and stance taking automatically.

We will first describe the corpus and the annotations. Next we look at the annotations of utterances consisting of starting with "yeah" and try to see whether we can classify these utterances as continuers, i.e. neutral with respect to stance taking (Schegloff, 1981), or as assessments.

2 Corpus

The argumentative discourses that we are studying are part of the meeting corpus collected during the AMI project (McCowan et al., 2005). From a computational, technological perspective, the aims

Proceedings of the Workshop on Embodied Language Processing, pages 17–24,
Prague, Czech Republic, June 28, 2007.

of this research is directed at developing automatic procedures that can help to provide answers to any query users may have about what goes on in the meetings. The AMI corpus consists of meetings in which a group of four people discuss the design of a new remote control. T

The kinds of queries that we would like our procedures to be able to answer are related to these moves: what suggestions have been made; what were the arguments given and how much animosity was there related to the decision. In the AMI corpus, the meeting recordings have been annotated on many levels, allowing the use of machine learning techniques to develop appropriate algorithms for answering such questions. We focus on the dialogue act annotation scheme. This contains three types of information. Information on the speech act, the relation between speech acts and information on addressing.

The dialogue act classes that are distinguished in our dialogue act annotation schema fall into the following classes:

- Classes for things that are not really dialogue acts at all, but are present to account for something in the transcription that doesn't really convey a speaker intention. This includes backchannels, stalls and fragments

- Classes for acts that are about information exchange: inform and elicit inform.

- Classes for acts about some action that an individual or group might take: suggest, offer, elicit suggest or offer.

- Classes for acts that are about commenting on the previous discussion: assess, comment about understanding, elicit assessment, elicit comment about understanding

- Classes for acts whose primary purpose is to smooth the social functioning of the group: be-positive, be-negative.

- A "bucket" type, OTHER, for acts that do convey a speaker intention, but where the intention doesn't fit any of the other classes.

For our studies into feedback in the AMI corpus, the dialogue acts labelled as backchannesl are clearly important. They were defined in the annotation manual as follows.

In backchannels, someone who has just been listening to a speaker says something in the background, without really stopping that speaker. [...] Some typical backchannels are "uhhuh", "mm-hmm", "yeah", "yep", "ok", "ah", "huh", "hmm", "mm" and, for the Scottish speakers in the data recorded in Edinburgh, "aye". Backchannels can also repeat or paraphrase part or all of what the main speaker has just said.

The labels *assess* and *comment-about-understanding* are closely related. They were defined as follows.

An ASSESS is any comment that expresses an evaluation, however tentative or incomplete, of something that the group is discussing. [...] There are many different kinds of assessment; they include, among other things, accepting an offer, expressing agreement/disagreement or any opinion about some information that's been given, expressing uncertainty as to whether a suggestion is a good idea or not, evaluating actions by members of the group, such as drawings. [...] An ASSESS can be very short, like "yeah" and "ok". It is important not to confuse this type of act with the class BACKCHANNEL, where the speaker is merely expressing, in the background, that they are following the conversation.

C-A-U is for the very specific case of commenting on a previous dialogue act where the speaker indicates something about whether they heard or understood what a previous speaker has said, without doing anything more substantive. In a C-A-U, the speaker can indicate either that they did understand (or simply hear) what a previous speaker said, or that they didn't.

The Backchannel class largely conforms to Yngve's notion of backchannel and is used for the functions of contact (Yngve, 1970). Assess is used for the attitudinal reactions, where the speaker expresses his stance towards what is said, either acceptance or rejection. Comments about understanding are used for explicit signals of understanding or non-understanding.

In addition to dialogue acts also relation between dialogue acts are annotated. Relations are annotated between two dialogue acts (a later source act and an earlier target act) or between a dialogue act (the source of the relation) and some other action, in which case the target is not specified. Relations are a more general concept than adjacency pairs, like question-answer. Relation have one of four types: positive, negative, partial and uncertain, indicating that the source expresses a positive, negative, partially positive or uncertain stance of the speaker towards the contents of the target of the related pair. For example: a "yes"-answer to a question is an inform act that is the source of a positive relation with the question act, which is the target of the relation. A dialogue act that assesses some action that is not a dialogue act, will be coded as the source of a relation that has no (dialogue act as) target.

A part of the scenario-based meetings (14 meetings) were annotated with addressee labels, i.e. annotators had to say who the speaker is talking to. The addressee tag is attached to the dialogue act. If a speaker changes his addressee (for instance, from group to a particular participant) during a turn the utterance should be split into two dialogue act segments, even if the type of dialogue act is the same for both segments.

3 Yeah

In this section we look at the distribution of *yeah* in the AMI corpus. "yeah" utterances make up a substantial part of the dialogue acts in the AMI meeting conversations (about 8%). If we try to tell group addressed dialogue acts from individually addressed acts then "yeah" is the best cue phrase for the class of single addressed dialogue acts; cf. (Stehouwer, 2006).

In order to get information about the stance that participants take with respect towards the issue discussed it is important to be able to tell utterances of "yeah" as a mere backchannel, or a stall, from yeah-utterances that express agreement with the opinion of the speaker. The latter will more often be classified as assessments. We first look at the way annotators used and confused the labels and then turn to see in what way we can predict the assignments to the class.

3.1 Annotations of yeah utterances

One important feature of the dialogue act annotation scheme is that the annotators had to decide what they consider to be the segments that constitute a dialogue act. Annotators differ in the way they segment the transcribed speech of a speaker. Where one annotator splits "Yeah. Maybe pear yeah or something like that." into two segments labeling "yeah." as a backchannel and the rest as a suggest, an other may not split it and consider the whole utterance as a suggest.

In comparing how different annotators labeled "yeah" occurrences, we compared the labels they assigned to the segment that starts with the occurrence of "yeah".

The confusion matrix for 2 annotators of 213 yeah-utterances, i.e. utterances that start with "yeah", is given below. It shows that backchannel (38%), assess (37%) and inform (11%) are the largest categories [1]. Each of the annotators has about 80 items in the backchannel class. In about 75% of the cases, annotators agree on the back-channel label. In either of the other cases a category deemed a backchannel is mostly categorized as assessment by the other and vice versa. For the assessments, annotators agree on about slightly more than half of the cases (43 out of 79 and 43 out of 76). The disagreements are, for both annotators split between the backchannels, for the larger part, the inform category, as second largest, and the **other** category.

The **other** category subsumes the following types of dialogue acts: summing up for both annotators: be-positive(9), suggest(8), elicit-assess(3), elicit-inform(2), comment-about-understanding(2). The dialogue act type of these **other** labeled utterances is mostly motivated by the utterances following "Yeah". Examples: "Yeah , it's a bit difficult" is labeled as Be-positive. "Yeah ? Was it a nice way to create your remote control ?" is labeled as an Elicit-Assessment .

Out of the 213 Yeah-utterances a number contains just "yeah" without a continuation. Below, the confusion matrix for the same two annotators, but now for only those cases that have text "yeah" only. In

[1] As the numbers for each of the classes by both annotators is about the same, we have permitted ourselves the license to this sloppy way of presenting the percentages.

yeah	0	1	2	3	4	SUM
0	59.0	2.0	17.0	0.0	2.0	80.0
1	0.0	9.0	4.0	2.0	2.0	17.0
2	21.0	3.0	43.0	7.0	5.0	79.0
3	2.0	0.0	7.0	13.0	4.0	26.0
4	1.0	0.0	5.0	0.0	5.0	11.0
SUM	83.0	14.0	76.0	22.0	18.0	213.0

Figure 1: Confusion matrix of two annotations of all Yeah utterances. labels: 0 = backchannel; 1 = fragment or stall; 2 = assess; 3 = inform; 4 = other. p0=0.61 (percentage agreement); kappa=0.44.

yeah-only	0	1	2	SUM
0	50.0	12.0	3.0	65.0
1	13.0	5.0	1.0	19.0
2	2.0	0.0	2.0	4.0
SUM	65.0	17.0	6.0	88.0

Figure 2: labels: 0 = bc 1 = assess 2 = other (subsuming: be-positive, fragment, comment-about-understanding). p0=0.65; kappa=0.14

the comparison only those segments were taken into account that both annotators marked as a segment i.e. a dialogue act realized by the word "Yeah" only.[2]

What do these patterns in the interpretation of "yeah" expressions tell us about its semantics? It appears that there is a significant collection of occurrences that annotators agree on as being backchannels. For the classes of assessments and other there also seem to be prototypical examples that are clear for both annotators. The confusions show that there is a class of expressions that are either interpreted as backchannel or assess and a class whose expressions are interpreted as either assessments or some other label. Annotators often disagree in segmentation. A segment of speech that only consist of the word "yeah" is considered to be either a backchannel or an assess, with very few exceptions. There is more confusion between annotators than agreement about the potential assess acts.

[2]The text segment covered by the dialogue act then contains "Yeah", "Yeah ?", "Yeah ," or "Yeah .".

3.2 Predicting the class of a yeah utterance

We derived a decision rule model for the assignment of a dialogue act label to yeah utterances, based on annotated meeting data. For our exploration we used decision tree classifiers as they have the advantage over other classifiers that the rules can be interpreted.

The data we used consisted of 1122 yeah utterances from 15 meetings. Because of the relative low inter-annotator agreement, we took meetings that were all annotated by one and the same annotator, because we expect that it will find better rules for classifying the utterances when the data is not too noisy.

There are 12786 dialogue act segments in the corpus. The number of segments that start with "yeah" is 1122, of which 861 are short utterances only containing the word "yeah". Of the 1122 yeahs 493 dialogue acts were annotated as related to a previous dialogue act. 319 out of the 861 short yeah utterances are related to a previous act.

The distribution of the 1122 yeah utterances over dialogue act classes is: assess (407), stall (224), backchannel (348), inform (95) and other (48 of which 25 comment-about-understanding). These are the class variables we used in the classification. The model consists of five features. We make use of the notion of *conversational state*, being an ensemble of the speech activities of all participants. Since we have four participants a state is a 4-tuple $< a, b, c, d >$ where a is the dialogue act performed by participant A, etc. A conversation is in a particular state as long as no participant stops or starts speaking. Thus, a state change occurs every time when some participants starts speaking or stops speaking, in the sense that the dialogue act that he performs has finished. The features that we use are:

- *lex* This feature has value 0 if the utterance consists of the word Yeah only. Otherwise 1.
- *continue* Has value 1 when the producer of the utterance also speaks in the next conversational state. Otherwise 0. This feature models incipient behavior of the backchanneler.
- *samespeaker* Has value 1 if the conversational state in which this utterance happens has the

Null	629.0
Assess	81.0
Inform	162.0
Elicit-Comment-Understanding	2.0
Elicit-Assessment	40.0
Elicit-Inform	73.0
Elicit-Offer-Or-Suggestion	2.0
Suggest	114.0
Comment-About-Understanding	13.0
Offer	5.0
Be-Positive	1.0

Figure 3: Distribution of the types of dialogue acts that yeah utterances are responses to.

same speaker, but different from the backchanneler, as the next state. Otherwise 0. This feature indicates that there is another speaker that continues speaking.

- *overlap* There is speaker overlap in the state where the utterance started.
- *source* This involves the relation labeling of the annotation scheme. *source* refers to the dialogue act type of the source of the relation of the dialogue act that is realized by the Yeah utterance. If the yeah dialogue act is not related to some other act the value of this feature is null. The possible values for this feature are: null, assess, inform, suggest, elicitation (which covers all elicitations), and other.

The distribution of source types of the 1122 yeah dialogue acts is shown in table 3.2. The table shows that 629 out of 1122 yeah utterances were not related to some other act.

We first show the decision tree computed by the J48-tree classifier as implemented in the weka-toolkit, if we do not use the source feature looks as follows. The tree shows that 392 utterances satisfy the properties: continued = 1 and short = 1. Of these 158 are misclassified as backchannel.

1. Continued ≤ 0
   (a) lex ≤ 0: bc(392.0/158.0)
   (b) lex > 0: as(56.0/24.0)
2. Continue $\rangle$ 0
   (a) samcspkr ≤ 0
      i. overlap ≤ 0: st(105.0/27.0)
      ii. overlap > 0
         A. lex ≤ 0: st(76.0/30.0)
         B. lex > 0: bc(16.0/6.0)
   (b) samespkr > 0 : ass(477.0/233.0)

In this case the J48 decision tree classifier has an accuracy of 57%. If we decide that every yeah utterance is a Backchannel, the most frequent class in our data, we would have an accuracy of 31%. If we include the source feature, so we know the type of dialogue act that the yeah utterance is a response to, the accuracy of the J48 classifier raises at 80%. Figure 3.2 shows the decision tree for this classifier. The results were obtained using ten-fold cross-validation.

It is clear from these results that there is a strong relation between the source type of a Yeah dialogue act and the way this Yeah dialogue act should be classified: as a backchannel or as an assess. Note that since backchannels are never marked as target of a relation, **null** as source value is a good indicator for the Yeah act to be a backchannel or a stall.

We also tested the decision tree classifier on a test set that consists of 4453 dialogue acts of which 539 are yeah-utterances (219 marked as related to some source act). Of these 219 are short utterances consisting only of the word "Yeah" (139 marked as related). The utterances in this test set were annotated by other annotators than the annotator that annotated the training set. The J48 classifier had an accuracy on the test set of 64%. The classes which are confused most are those that are also confused most by the human annotators: backchannels and stall, and assess and inform. One cause of the performance drop is that in the test corpus the distribution of class labels differs substantially from that of the training set. In the test set yeah utterances were very rarely labelled as stall, whereas this was a frequent label (about 20%) in the training set. The distribution of yeah-utterance labels in the test set is: backchannels 241, stalls 4, assessments 186, inform 66 and other 42.

When we merged the train and test meetings and trained the J48 decision tree classifier, a 10 fold cross-validation test showed an accuracy of 75%. Classes that are confused most are again: backchannel and stall, and assessment and inform.

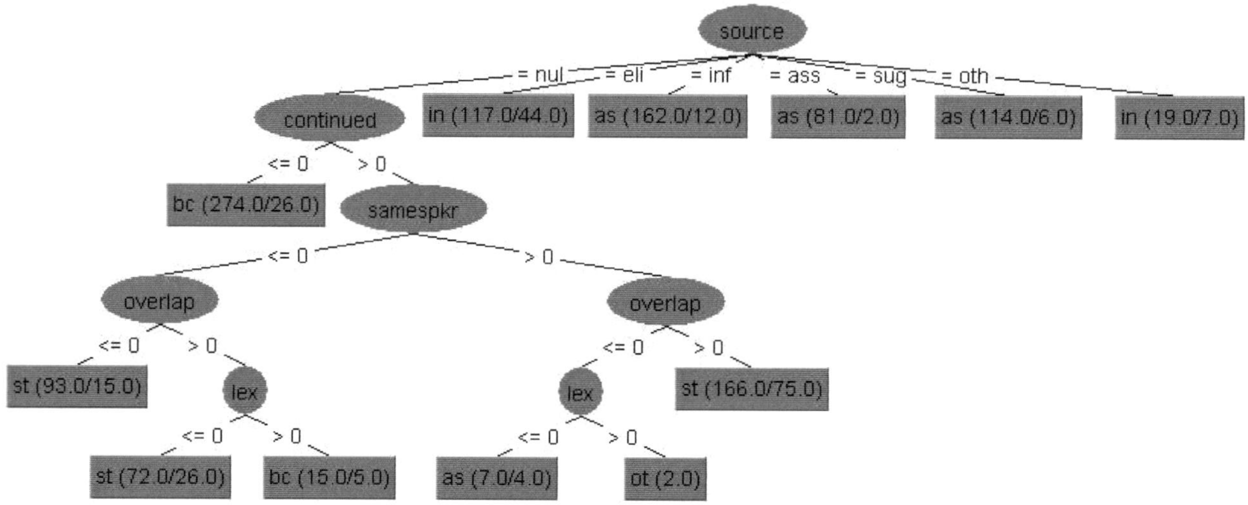

Figure 4: Decision tree for classification of yeah utterances when information about the source of the related dialogue act is used.

4 Measuring Speaker Gaze at Backchannelors

When thinking about the interaction between speaker and backchannelor, it seems obvious, as we said before, that the person backchanneling feels addressed by the speaker. We were wondering whether the backchannel was not prompted by an invitation of a speaker, for example, by gazing at the listener.

Gaze behavior of speaker and backchannelor is classified by means of the following gaze targets, a sequence of focus of attention labels that indicates where the actor is looking at during a period of time:

1. the gaze targets of the *speaker* in the period starting some short time ($DeltaTime$) before the start time of the backchannel act till the start of the backchannel act.

2. the gaze targets of the *backchannelor* in the period starting some short time ($DeltaTime$) before the start time of the backchannel act till the start of the backchannel act.

3. the gaze targets of the speaker during the backchannel act.

4. the gaze targets of the backchannelor during the backchannel act.

We set $DeltaTime$ at 1 sec, so we observed the gaze behavior of the speaker in the period from one second before the start of the backchannel act. Using these gaze target sequences, we classified the gaze behavior of the actor as follows:

0: the gaze before target sequence of the actor does not contain any person

1: the before gaze target sequence of the actor does contain a person but not the other actor involved: for the speaker this means that he did not look at backchannelor before the backchannel act started, for the backchannelor this means that he did not look at the speaker before the start of the backchannel.

2: the actor did look at the other person involved before that backchannel act.

Figure 4 show a table with counts of these classes of events. In the 13 meetings we counted 1085 backchannel events. There were 687 events with a single speaker of a real dialogue act. For this cases it is clear who the backchannelor was reacting on. This is the selected speaker. The table shows speaker data in rows and backchannel data in columns. The $MaxDownTime$ is $1sec$ and the $MinUpTime$ is 2 sec. The $DeltaTime$ for the gaze period is $1sec$. From the table we can infer that:

1. The selected speaker looks at the backchannelor in the period before the backchannelor act starts in 316 out of the 687 cases.

2. The backchannelor looks at the selected speaker in the period before the backchannelor act starts in 430 out of the 687 cases.

3. The selected speaker looks at someone else than the backchannelor in the period before the backchannelor act starts in 209 out of the 687 cases.

4. The backchannelor looks at someone else than the selected speaker in the period before the backchannelor act starts in 54 out of the 687 cases.

5. In 254 out of the 687 cases the speaker looked at the backchannelor and the backchannelor looked at the speaker.

We may conclude that the speakers look more at the backchannelor than at the other two persons together (316 against 209). The table also shows that backchannelors look far more at the selected speaker than at the two others (430 against 54 instances).

In order to compare gaze of speaker in backchannel events, we also computed for each of the 13 meetings for each pair of participants (X, Y): $dagaze(X, Y)$: how long X looks at Y in those time frames that X is performing a dialogue act.

$$dagaze(X, Y) = \frac{\sum OT(gaze(X, Y), da(X))}{\sum da(X)} \tag{1}$$

where summation is over all real dialogue acts performed by X,
$OT(gaze(X, Y), da(X))$ is the overlap time of the

$sp\|bc$	0	1	2	T
0	103	4	55	162
1	46	42	121	209
2	54	8	254	316
T	203	54	430	687

Figure 5: Gaze table of speaker and backchannelor. $DeltaTime = 1sec$. Total number of backchannel events is 1085. In the table only those 687 backchannel events with a single speaker are considered (excluded are those instances where no speaker or more than one speaker was performing a real dialogue act in the period with a $MinUpTime$ of 2 sec and a $MaxDownTime$ of 1 sec.). Speaker data in rows; backchannelor data in columns. The table shows for example that in 121 cases the speaker looked at someone but not the backchannelor, in the period from 1 sec before the start of the backchannel act till the start of the backchannel act, while the backchannelor looked in that period at the speaker.

two events: $gaze(X, Y)$: the time that X gazes at Y, and $da(X)$ the time that the dialogue act performed by X lasts. The numbers are normalized over the total duration of the dialogue acts during which gaze behavior was measured.

Next we computed $bcgaze(X, Y)$: how long X looks at Y in those time frames that X performs a real dialogue act and the Y responds with a backchannel act.

$$bcgaze(X, Y) = \frac{\sum OT(gaze(X, Y), dabc(X, Y))}{\sum da(X, Y)} \tag{2}$$

where $dabc(X, Y)$ is the time that X performs the dialogue act that Y reacts on by a backchannel. Here normalization is with the sum of the lengths of all dialogue acts performed by X that elicited a backchannel act by Y.

Analysis of pairs of values $gaze(X, Y)$ and $bcgaze(X, Y)$ shows that in a situation where someone performs a backchannel the speaker looks significantly more at the backchannelor than the speaker looks at the same person in general when the speaker is performing a dialogue act ($t = 8.66$, $df = 101$, $p < 0.0001$). The mean values are 0.33

and 0.16.[3]

Perhaps we can use the information on gaze of the participants in the short period before the backchannel act as features for predicting who the backchannel actor is. For the 687 data points of backchannel events with a single speaker, we used gaze of participants, the speaker and the duration of the backchannel act as features. Using a decision tree classifier we obtained an accuracy of 51% in predicting who will perform a backchannel act (given that someone will do that). Note that there are three possible actors (the speaker is given). This score is 16% above the a priori likelihood of the most likely participant: A (36%).

Conclusion

In this paper, we have explored some questions about the possible use and function of backchannels in multiparty interactions. On the one hand backchannels can be informative about functions related to floor and participation: who is talking to whom. Obviously, a person producing a backchannel was responding to an utterance of speaker. For the semantic analysis of meeting data an important question is whether he was just using the backchannel as a continuer (a sign of attention) or as an assessment. We also checked our intuition that backchannels in the kinds of meetings that we are looking at might often be invited by speakers through gaze. Obviously, these investigations just scratch the service of how backchannels work in conversations and how we can use them to uncover information from recorded conversations.

References

H. H. Clark and T. B. Carlson. 1992. Hearers and speech acts. In Herbert H. Clark, editor, *Arenas of Language Use*, pages 205–247. University of Chicago Press and CSLI.

Erving Goffman. 1981. Footing. In Erving Goffman, editor, *Forms of Talk*, pages 124–159. University of Pennsylvania Press, Philadelphia, PA.

Stephen C. Levinson. 1988. Putting linguistics on a proper footing: explorations in goffman's concept of participation. In Paul Drew and Anthony Wootton, editors, *Erving Goffman. Exploring the Interaction Order*, pages 161–227. Polity Press, Cambridge.

I. McCowan, J. Carletta, W. Kraaij, S. Ashby, S. Bourban, M. Flynn, M. Guillemot, T. Hain, J. Kadlec, V. Karaiskos, M.Kronenthal, G. Lathoud, M. Lincoln, A. Lisowska, W. Post, D. Reidsma, and P. Wellner. 2005. The ami meeting corpus. In *Measuring Behaviour, Proceedings of 5th International Conference on Methods and Techniques in Behavioral Research.*

Emanuel A. Schegloff. 1981. Discourse as an interactional achievement: some uses of 'uh huh' and other things that come between sentences. In Deborah Tannen, editor, *Analyzing Discourse: Text and Talk*, pages 71–93. Georgetown University Press, Washington.

Emanuel A. Schegloff. 1988. Goffman and the analysis of conversation. In Paul Drew and Anthony Wootton, editors, *Erving Goffman. Exploring the Interaction Order*, pages 89–135. Polity Press, Cambridge.

J.H. Stehouwer. 2006. Cue-phrase selection methods for textual classification problems. Technical report, M.Sc. Thesis, Twente University, Human Media Interaction, Enschede, the Netherlands.

V.H. Yngve. 1970. On getting a word in edgewise. In *Papers from the sixth regional meeting of the Chicago Linguistic Society*, pages 567–77, Chicago: Chicago Linguistic Society.

[3]For 13 meeting and 4 participants we would have 156 pairs of values. We only used those 102 pairs of which both values are non-zero.

Which way to turn? Guide orientation in virtual way finding

Mark Evers
Technical & Professional Communication
University of Twente
The Netherlands
M.Evers@alumnus.utwente.nl

Mariët Theune
Human Media Interaction
University of Twente
The Netherlands
M.Theune@utwente.nl

Joyce Karreman
Technical & Professional Communication
University of Twente
The Netherlands
J.Karreman@utwente.nl

Abstract

In this paper we describe an experiment aimed at determining the most effective and natural orientation of a virtual guide that gives route directions in a 3D virtual environment. We hypothesized that, due to the presence of mirrored gestures, having the route provider directly face the route seeker would result in a less effective and less natural route description than having the route provider adapt his orientation to that of the route seeker. To compare the effectiveness of the different orientations, after having received a route description the participants in our experiment had to 'virtually' traverse the route using prerecorded route segments. The results showed no difference in effectiveness between the two orientations, but suggested that the orientation where the speaker directly faces the route seeker is more natural.

1 Introduction

When someone approaches us and asks which way to go, we naturally turn – if necessary – so we face the direction to take (which makes it also easier for ourselves to imagine traversing the route). Generally, the route seeker then also turns to adapt his or her orientation to match ours, and we end up sharing the same perspective on the route to take.[1] Presumably, this matching of physical orientation is meant to reduce the mental effort that is involved in matching another person's perspective on a spatial scene for both speaker and hearer (Shelton and McNamara, 2004). However, someone who faces an embodied virtual agent presenting a route description in a virtual environment (projected on a computer screen) cannot turn to match his or her perspective with that of the agent, as turning away from the screen would result in losing sight of both the agent and the virtual environment. In this situation, the only way to bring the perspectives of route provider (agent) and route seeker (user) closer together is for the agent to adapt its orientation to match that of the user. In this paper, we describe an experiment carried out to determine if such a change in orientation by the route provider helps the route seeker with virtual way finding. Although the experiment was aimed at determining the most effective and natural orientation of a Virtual Guide, we used prerecorded route descriptions presented by a human route provider. The Virtual Guide that we have developed (see next section) was still being implemented at the time.

2 The Virtual Guide

We have developed an embodied Virtual Guide[2] that can give route directions in a 3D environment, which is a virtual reality replica of a public building in our home town. When navigating through this virtual environment, shown on the computer screen from a first person perspective, the user can approach the Virtual Guide to ask for directions. Currently the

[1]This observation is based on personal experience. We also observed this behaviour in a small corpus of route description video's.

[2]See http://wwwhome.cs.utwente.nl/~hofs/dialogue for an online demo.

Proceedings of the Workshop on Embodied Language Processing, pages 25–32,
Prague, Czech Republic, June 28, 2007.

Guide is behind the reception desk (see Figure 1), but she can be situated anywhere in the building.

The first part of the interaction between the Virtual Guide and the user consists of a natural language dialogue in which the Guide tries to find out the user's intended destination. This may involve subdialogues, in which either the Guide or the user asks the other for clarification, and the resolution of anaphoric expressions (e.g., *How do I get there?*). Input and output modalities include text, speech and pointing. For an in-depth description of the dialogue module of the Virtual Guide, see Hofs et al. (2003).

When the user's destination has been established, the Virtual Guide gives a natural language route description, in the form of a monologue that cannot be interrupted. This is somewhat unnatural since in real direction giving, the route seeker tends to give feedback and, if necessary, ask for clarification while the route is being described. However, since in our system dialogue management and the generation of route descriptions are handled by separate, specialised modules this is currently not possible.

The route is presented as a sequence of segments, which are mostly expressed as "point+direction" combinations (Dale et al., 2005). That is, they consist of a turn direction combined with the location where this turn is to be made, specified in terms of a landmark. For example, *You go left at the information sign*. The route description is generated as follows. First, the shortest path between starting point and destination is computed based on predefined paths in the virtual environment. Turn directions are derived from the relative angles of subsequent path segments, and landmarks are selected based on their relative salience (e.g., in terms of size or colour) and proximity to a turning point. The sequence of turn directions and associated landmarks is then given as input to the natural language generation component, which is based on Exemplars (White and Caldwell, 1998). After a first version of the route description has been generated using a collection of standard sentence structures, this initial description is revised by randomly aggregating some sentences and adding cue phrases such as *and then*, *after that* etc. to achieve some variation in the generated text.

To generate appropriate gestures to accompany the verbal route description, the generated text is extended with tags associating the words in the route description with different types of gestures. Currently this is done using a simple keyword approach. Direction words (*left, right*) are associated with pointing gestures in the corresponding directions, and references to landmarks are associated with deictic gestures pointing to either the absolute or the relative location of these objects (see Section 3). Some iconic gestures (i.e., gestures that have a resemblance in shape to what they depict) are also available, for example a horizontal tube-like gesture that can be used in references to corridors and tunnels. Unlike the pointing gestures, which are generated "on the fly", the iconic gestures of the Virtual Guide are generated by using canned animations. For a more sophisticated approach to the generation of iconic gestures, see the work by Kopp et al. (in press) who describe the dynamic planning of novel iconic gestures by NUMACK, an embodied conversational agent that functions as a virtual guide for the Northwestern University campus.

Figure 1: The Virtual Guide.

The last stage of the route description process in our Virtual Guide is to send the marked-up text to the animation planner, which actually generates the required animations in synchronization with text-to-speech output. The animation planner is based on the work by Welbergen et al. (2006).

3 The Guide's gestures and orientation

During the route description, the Virtual Guide can make pointing gestures from either an 'objective' viewpoint, i.e., pointing at the absolute locations of objects, or from a 'character' viewpoint, i.e., pointing at locations relative to the position of a person who is walking the route. An objective viewpoint makes most sense when pointing at objects that are (in principle) visible to both the agent and the user, which is only the case for objects that are located at the start of the route. So, most of the time the Guide will be using the character viewpoint, pointing left and right relative to its own body to indicate landmarks and directions from the perspective of someone who is walking along the route being described.

The typical orientation of information presenting agents is facing the user. However, it is not a priori clear that this would be the best option for the Virtual Guide. When facing the user, all pointing gestures made by the guide from a character viewpoint would mirrored in the eyes of the user, so the latter would have to perform a mental 180° re-orientation of the gestures. This would demand extra cognitive effort on top of processing and storing the verbally presented route information, and might negatively influence the user's ability to reproduce the route directions during actual traversal of the route.

In actual direction giving situations, people often tend to minimize the difference in orientation between them. Therefore we wondered if reducing the difference in orientation between the agent and the user would help the user to find his way during traversal. If the agent would turn to face almost the same direction as the user, its gestures could be expressed as close to the route seeker's perspective as possible, thus reducing the cognitive load for the user in processing them. Also, we wondered if this configuration would yield a more natural effect than having the agent directly face the user during the route description. We investigated these questions in an experiment where participants had to virtually follow a route, presented to them in one of two versions that differed in the orientation of the route provider. Because the Virtual Guide was still being implemented at the time, we used route descriptions by a human route provider. The experimental setup and its results are presented below, followed by some conclusions and future research directions.

4 The orientation experiment

The goal of the experiment was to investigate the effect of speaker orientation on the effectiveness and naturalness of a route description. For our experiment, we opted to use prerecorded route descriptions, as this matched the capabilities of our Virtual Guide (which can only present the route as a monologue with no interaction) and also ensured an unlimited number of reproductions of constant quality and content. We recorded two separate route descriptions that differed in speaker orientation with respect to the route seeker, but were otherwise (largely) the same:

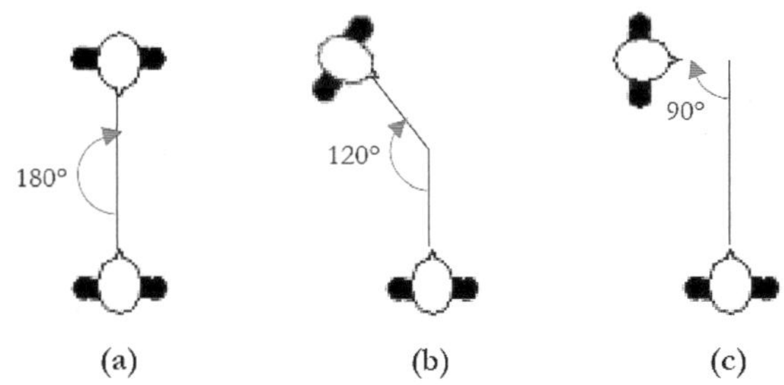

Figure 2: Angle between route provider and route seeker (camera)

180° version The route provider is oriented at a 180° angle with respect to the route seeker, i.e., he directly faces the camera lens, creating mirrored gestures (his left is seen as right by the viewer and vice versa). See Figures 2(a) and 3(a).

120° version The route provider is oriented at a 120° angle toward the route seeker, as if to adapt his orientation to that of the route seeker. See Figures 2(b) and 3(b).

We chose an orientation of 120° for the route seeker-oriented version, so as to maintain visibility of non-verbal signals. If the route provider were to assume an orientation of 90° or less, as illustrated in Figure 2(c), not all gestures would be visible and maintaining eye contact could make his posture unnatural.

The 120° and the 180° condition only differed in bodily orientation while eye contact remained unchanged and facial expressions remained visible. Also, although wording slightly varied, the presented information was the same in both conditions. The route descriptions were recorded on location in a small town with short streets and plenty

a)  b) 

Figure 3: "Turn left at the white building" (a: 180°, b: 120°)

of landmarks. The route being described led from the recording location to the town hotel. The verbal description was similar in structure to those generated by the Virtual Guide. It mentioned five decision points, each connected with one or two characteristic landmarks. For example, *At the men's fashion shop, you turn right.* During the route description, the route provider made beat gestures and pointing gestures from a character viewpoint, taking his own body orientation as a reference for left and right. Apart from a few slight variations, the gestures used in both versions of the route description were the same; see Figure 3. At the start of the route description, both route provider and route seeker were exactly (180° version) or almost (120° version) perpendicular to the starting direction of the route.

After viewing one of the two versions of the route description, the participants in the experiment had to 'virtually traverse' the route (to measure effectiveness of the route description) and were asked how natural they found the route description. The most realistic way to measure effectiveness of the route description would have been to have the participants walk the route in reality after having received the description, as was done by Fujii et al. (2000) and Michon and Denis (2001). However, conducting such an experiment is a very time consuming activity. As a more practical alternative we developed a reconstructive method allowing participants to traverse the route on the computer, instead of in a real (live) environment. In this set-up, participants 'traversed' the route by viewing prerecorded route segments, showing a moving scene from a first person perspective as if they walked through the streets themselves, accompanied by street sounds. Apart from practical considerations, an additional advantage of this set-up is that it yields full control with respect to repeatability and the participation setting because of its playback nature.

Our hypotheses were as follows:

1. The 120° version is more effective, i.e., yields a more successful traversal than its 180° counterpart.

2. The 120° version yields a more natural route description than its 180° counterpart.

4.1 Participants

A total of 49 participants were involved in the experiment, aged 20 to 64 years (with an average of 33 years). Since no participants were younger than 12 or post 70, no specific effect of age on their spatial skills was expected (Hunt and Waller, 1999). Since gender is an influential factor in orientation and way finding (Hunt and Waller, 1999; Lawton, 1994), we used a 50% male - 50% female test population. The 120° version of the route description was shown to 13 male and 12 female participants; the 180° version to 11 male and 13 female participants.

4.2 Procedure

The experiment consisted of the following steps.

Introduction - After reading an introductory text explaining the experiment, the participant filled in a pre-questionnaire asking for age, gender, and educational level. We also asked how familiar the participant was with the route location, indicated on a

5-point scale ranging from not at all familiar (1) to very familiar (5). If the participant indicated being moderately or more familiar with the location, his or her results were discarded. The questionnaire was followed by an example question to familiarize the participant with the controls and with the set-up of the traversal part of the experiment.

Route description - First, the participant was shown a video impression of the location where he or she, being lost in an unfamiliar town, supposedly approached someone to ask the way to the hotel. Then the participant watched one of the two prerecorded route descriptions. To compensate for the fact that, unlike a real-life situation, there was no opportunity to verify understanding or ask for clarifications, the participants were allowed to play the route description video twice.

Traversal - After having received the route description, the participant had to virtually traverse the route by watching six prerecorded traversal segments in succession, appearing in a pop-up window. The first segment began at the starting point of the route and ended at the first decision point (intersection). Each following segment started where the previous one ended, with the final segment ending at the destination of the route. At the end of each route segment, an overview of the next intersection was provided by moving the camera viewpoint gradually so the entire intersection was shown. The average length of each traversal segment was around 1.5 minutes.

After watching each segment, the participant had to select which direction to take next from a limited set of options: left, straight ahead or right (if applicable). Each option was accompanied with a photo of the corresponding view from the crossing. After answering the question, the participant was informed which direction was correct. Then the participant proceeded with the route traversal from the correct turn, regardless whether the correct direction had been chosen or not.[3]

[3]This differs from the effectiveness measure of Fujii et al. (2000), who used a movement failure rate defined as Out/N, with Out being the number of times a participant lost the way and was unable to return to the route, and N being the number of trials. We found this method too complicated in design and too confusing for the participants to be used in this experiment. In our set-up, the participant was only allowed one trial per decision point and always traveled along the correct route.

	120°	180°	Total
Male	3.46 (0.88)	3.27 (1.19)	3.38 (1.01)
Female	4.00 (1.04)	3.62 (0.77)	3.80 (0.91)
Total	3.72 (0.98)	3.46 (0.98)	3.59 (0.98)

Table 1: Number of correct decisions as a function of gender and version (results are presented as Means with Std. Deviations in brackets).

Post-questionnaire - After route traversal, the participants answered several questions about the route description. Here we only focus on one of the questions, i.e., "Do you think the route provider described the route in a natural way?", to be answered on a 5-point scale ranging from very natural (1) to very artificial (5). The participants were also offered the opportunity to comment on their answer.

5 Results and discussion

Here we present and discuss the main findings from our experiment.

5.1 Effectiveness of the route description

Hypothesis 1 concerned the influence of speaker orientation on the effectiveness of the route description. We measured this by counting the number of correct turns taken by the participants during route traversal. The route contained five decision points (intersections), so participants' scores ranged from 0 to 5 correct turns. Gender has been proved to strongly influence way finding ability (Hunt and Waller, 1999; Lawton, 1994), so gender was accounted for as a fixed factor in our analysis.

The results are summarized in Table 1, which shows that participants performed slightly better in the 120° version than in the 180° version, and that women performed slightly better than men. However, these differences were not significant; neither for version nor gender. Thus, our first hypothesis is not supported.

This lack of effect might be taken as evidence that gestures hardly play a role in conveying information, so that a difference in their orientation would not affect the route seeker's mental processing of the route description. It has been argued that the main function of gestures in conversation is not to transfer information to the interlocutor, but to facilitate the cognitive process of speaking

(Rimé and Schiaratura, 1991; Morsella and Krauss, 2004). Still, though most spontaneous gestures may not be produced for the interlocutor's benefit, it has been shown experimentally that people do make use of the information conveyed by gestures (Kendon, 1994; Cassell et al., 1999; Kelly et al., 1999). The communicative power of gestures does seem to depend on the task and the type of gesture, however (Bangerter and Chevalley, 2007). In fact, in our experiment the gestures were not essential for understanding the route description. All pointing gestures were accompanied by explicit verbal descriptions of the corresponding landmarks and/or directions; in other words, the gestures were redundant with respect to speech. So, regarded from a purely informational point of view, these gestures were superfluous and the participants may have paid only limited attention to them or even consciously ignored them. This explanation is supported by the comments of various participants who said they tried to focus on the verbal instructions because the description was extensive and they found the gestures distracting.

We consciously limited the number of decision points in the experiment to five, well within the 7±2 range of short term memory, but for each decision point the route provider not only mentioned the direction to take, but also one or two landmarks. Furthermore, he gave some auxiliary hints of what to do in-between turns (*Walk straight ahead until you see a traffic sign; there you keep walking straight ahead*) and some more details. In their comments, several participants mentioned being distracted by too much detail in the description, and said they found the directions hard to remember. As a consequence, some participants tended to ignore the gestures or look away from the computer screen altogether. Obviously, doing so would clearly impair the effect of speaker orientation to be demonstrated by the experiment. On the other hand, not all participants ignored the gestures (at least not initially) as in the 180° version, some participants declared that they found the mirrored gestures annoying.

5.2 Naturalness of the route description

In Table 2, test results on the naturalness of the route description are shown for speaker orientation and gender. Orientation had an almost-significant effect on participants' judgement of naturalness (two-way ANOVA; $F(1,45)=3.35$, $p=0.07$ two-tailed).[4] The effect would have been significant if it had been the other way around. The effect of gender was not significant, and neither was the interaction of version and gender.

Contrary to our hypothesis, the participants judged the 180° version as being more natural than the 120° version. This was contrary to what was expected, because 'in the real world' route providers and seekers tend to minimize the difference in their orientation. In fact, as mentioned above, several participants reported being annoyed by the mirrored gestures in the 180° version. These contradictory findings suggest that it was not the route provider's gestures or their orientation that were crucial for the judgement on naturalness, but only whether the route provider's body was fully turned toward his audience – directly addressing them – or not. This may be the result of many previous confrontations with presenters (human or other) displayed on television or computer screens, explaining things to an audience. Perhaps the natural tendency to make orientations as similar as possible when explaining a route to someone does not transfer to a situation where the route is presented by somebody on a screen: a form of presentation in which we expect someone to be facing us.

Furthermore, the fixed position of the camera during the route description may also have interfered with its naturalness. If the route provider points into some direction, we tend to turn our heads to that direction, maybe in the assumption he will point at some landmark that can help us orientate or navigate. The fixed position of the camera, in contrast with the adaptive orientation of the route provider, may have yielded an unnatural combination in the case of the 120° version of the route description.

5.3 Gender effects

For both versions of the route description, women performed better than men. Although not significant, the difference in performance is sufficiently remarkable to merit some discussion. We believe the difference may be explained by the fact that women and men employ different strategies for way find-

[4] A two-tailed test was performed in spite of our one-sided hypothesis 2, because the effect was contrary to what was expected.

	120°	180°	Total
Male	2.62 (1.26)	1.73 (0.91)	2.21 (1.18)
Female	2.75 (1.14)	2.46 (1.13)	2.60 (1.12)
Total	2.68 (1.18)	2.13 (1.08)	2.41 (1.15)

Table 2: Naturalness as a function of gender and version (results are presented as Means with Std. Deviations in brackets).

ing (Hunt and Waller, 1999): women's strategies are most suited for tracking and piloting, whereas men use strategies appropriate for navigation. Tracking is a point-to-point way finding strategy that relies on information limited to environmental characteristics along the route. Piloting combines these environmental characteristics with self-centered orientation and direction (e.g., "When you're facing the main entrance, turn to the right"). Navigation, on the other hand, uses configurational information: routes are derived from knowledge of the surroundings of the destination or its global position. Thus, men tend to pay attention to bearings while women often rely on descriptions of control points and cues to the route such as landmarks (Lawton, 1994).

Looking at the set-up of our experiment, we see that it seems to favour a strategy of point-to-point decision making instead of relying on a more general and global sense of direction, as in navigation. First, the route description consisted entirely of landmarks to identify decision points and turns to be made when encountering them, fitting a tracking and piloting approach to way finding. Second, both the route description and the traversal segments were shown on a screen, with a restricted and forced field of vision. This may have impeded the estimation of global position, direction and distance, i.e., the kind of spatial knowledge men rely on for orientation and way finding. So, the way finding strategy that women already tend to employ in everyday life may have been most suited to this experiment and hence their higher score.

6 Conclusions and future work

The goal of this study was to find out which orientation of the Virtual Guide would be most effective and natural for providing route descriptions in a virtual environment. To test effectiveness, we devised a method that allowed participants to 'virtually' traverse a route by watching pre-recorded route segments and making turn decisions at intersections. We hypothesized that a speaker orientation of 120° with respect to the route seeker would result in a more effective and natural route description than a 180° orientation, because it would take the route seeker less effort to match the speaker's gestures with his or her own perspective. However, we found no effect of speaker orientation on task performance. A possible explanation lies in the complexity of our route description, which caused some participants to focus only on the verbal part of the description. Contrary to our expectation, the 180° orientation was judged to be more natural, in spite of the fact that some participants found the mirrored gestures annoying. The reason for this may be that people expect a speaker to be directly facing them when presenting information on a screen.

Based on these results, we decided to stick to the standard 180° orientation for our Virtual Guide. However, some reservations are in order when applying the results of our study to the Virtual Guide. For one thing, the route descriptions used in the experiment were not given by an agent but by a real human, albeit pre-recorded. This is still far from the situation in which an embodied agent is communicating with a user by means of an interface. A second difference with the Virtual Guide lies in the participant's navigational control. In the context of the Virtual Guide, the user can actively navigate through, and look around in, the environment to be traversed. In our experiment, the participants' view was restricted and forced by that of the camera which severely restricted their possibilities for orientation and navigation.

An obvious line of future research is therefore to repeat our experiment with the Virtual Guide, and have participants actually traverse the route by navigating through the 3D virtual environment, with total freedom of movement. This will make the traversal part more realistic and also more suitable for male way finding strategies, thus providing a better and more neutral measure for the effectiveness of the route description. In addition, we expect that the participants will be less inclined to see the guide as a kind of TV presenter and more as a real presence, because they will (virtually) share the same 3D environment with it. This may lead the participants to be less biased toward a 180° orientation of the route provider. Finally, all information not strictly necessary for way finding will be left out of the route description. This includes landmarks located along traversal segments rather than at intersections, and instructions to go 'straight ahead' (which several participants found confusing in the current experiment). With a less complex description, participants may refrain from ignoring the gestures made by the route provider and thereby be more susceptible to manipulation of speaker orientation.

Acknowledgements

The authors would like to thank Mark Tempelman and Job van den Wildenberg for their help with the experiment. The Virtual Guide was implemented by Dennis Hofs, Rieks op den Akker, Marco van Kessel, Richard Korthuis and Martin Bouman. The research reported here was carried out within the context of the project ANGELICA (A Natural-language Generator for Embodied, Lifelike Conversational Agents) sponsored by the Netherlands Organisation for Scientific Research, NWO (grant number 532.001.301).

References

A. Bangerter and E. Chevalley. 2007. Pointing and describing in referential communication: When are pointing gestures used to communicate? In *Proceedings of the Workshop on Multimodal Output Generation (MOG 2007)*, pages 17–28.

J. Cassell, D. McNeill, and K.E. McCullough. 1999. Speech-gesture mismatches: Evidence for one underlying representation of linguistic and non-linguistic information. *Pragmatics and Cognition*, 7(1):1–33.

R. Dale, S. Geldof, and J. Prost. 2005. Using natural language generation in automatic route description. *Journal of Research and Practice in Information Technology*, 37(1):89–105.

K. Fujii, S. Nagai, Y. Miyazaki, and K. Sugiyama. 2000. Navigation support in a real city using city metaphors. In T. Ishida and K. Isbister, editors, *Digital Cities*, Lecture Notes in Computer Science 1765, pages 338–349. Springer-Verlag, Berlin Heidelberg.

D. Hofs, R. op den Akker, and A. Nijholt. 2003. A generic architecture and dialogue model for multimodal interaction. In P. Paggio, K. Jokinen, and A. Jnsson, editors, *Proceedings of the 1st Nordic Symposium on Multimodal Communication*, volume 1, pages 79–91, Copenhagen. CST Publication, Center for Sprogteknologi.

E. Hunt and D. Waller. 1999. Orientation and wayfinding: A review. ONR technical report N00014-96-0380, Office of Naval Research, Arlington, VA.

S. D. Kelly, D. Barr, R.B. Church, and K. Lynch. 1999. Offering a hand to pragmatic understanding: The role of speech and gesture in comprehension and memory. *Journal of Memory and Language*, 40:577–592.

A. Kendon. 1994. Do gestures communicate? a review. *Research on Language and Social Interaction*, 27(3):175–200.

S. Kopp, P. Tepper, K. Striegnitz, and J. Cassell. in press. Trading spaces: How humans and humanoids use speech and gesture to give directions. In T. Nishida, editor, *Engineering Approaches to Conversational Informatics*. John Wiley and Sons.

C.A. Lawton. 1994. Gender differences in wayfinding strategies: Relationship to spatial ability and spatial anxiety. *Sex Roles*, 30(11-12):765–779.

P. Michon and M. Denis. 2001. When and why are visual landmarks used in giving directions? In D.R. Montello, editor, *Spatial Information Theory. Foundations of Geographic Information Science: International Conference, COSIT 2001*, Lecture Notes in Computer Science 2205, pages 292–305. Springer-Verlag, Berlin Heidelberg.

E. Morsella and R. Krauss. 2004. The role of gestures in spatial working memory and speech. *American Journal of Psychology*, 117(3):251–270.

B. Rimé and L. Schiaratura. 1991. Gesture and speech. In R. Feldman and B. Rimé, editors, *Fundamentals of Nonverbal Behavior*, pages 239–281. Cambridge University Press, Cambridge.

A.L. Shelton and T.P. McNamara. 2004. Spatial memory and perspective taking. *Memory and Cognition*, 32(3):416–426.

H. van Welbergen, A. Nijholt, D. Reidsma, and J. Zwiers. 2006. Presenting in virtual worlds: Towards an architecture for a 3d presenter explaining 2d-presented information. *IEEE Intelligent Systems*, 21(5):47–53.

M. White and T. Caldwell. 1998. EXEMPLARS: A practical, extensible framework for dynamic text generation. In *Proceedings of the Ninth International Workshop on Natural Language Generation*, pages 266–275.

A "person" in the interface: effects on user perceptions of multibiometrics

Álvaro Hernández, Beatriz López, David Díaz, Rubén Fernández, Luis Hernández
GAPS, Signal, Systems and Radiocommunications Department
Universidad Politécnica de Madrid
Ciudad Universitaria s/n, 28040 Madrid, Spain
alvaro@gaps.ssr.upm.es

Javier Caminero
Multilinguism & Speech Technology Group
Telefónica I+D
Emilio Vargas,6, 28043,Madrid,Spain
fjcg@tid.es

Abstract

In this paper we explore the possibilities that conversational agent technology offers for the improvement of the quality of human-machine interaction in a concrete area of application: the multimodal biometric authentication system. Our approach looks at the user perception effects related to the system interface rather than to the performance of the biometric technology itself. For this purpose we have created a multibiometric user test environment with two different interfaces or interaction metaphors: one with an embodied conversational agent and the other with on-screen text messages only. We present the results of an exploratory experiment that reveals interesting effects, related to the presence of a conversational agent, on the user's perception of parameters such as privacy, ease of use, invasiveness or system security.

1 Introduction

The term biometrics, in Information Technology, refers to an array of techniques to identify people based on one or more unique behavioural or physiological characteristics. The techniques themselves have improved considerably over the past few decades, in terms of performance and reliability, with reported error rates at levels that indicate a reasonable level of technological maturity (Wayman et al., 2005). But in order to be truly useful the technology has to be acceptable to people in each of its areas of application. It is widely recognised (BioSec, 2004) that to achieve this goal a user-centred understanding much deeper than that which we have today is needed, and one which encompasses the important problem of interaction with the interface. These, of course, are basic goals of the more general field of Human-Computer Interaction, added to which are more specific issues regarding security (Sasse, 2004).

As regards application interface technology, ever more realistic animated characters or embodied conversational agents (ECAs) are being gradually introduced in the hope that they will enhance the users' experience and enrich the interaction. Some applications of ECAs promise to bring us closer to achieving universal usability. For instance, they can be used to communicate with hearing impaired people through sign language (Huenerfauth, 2005) or lip-reading (Beskow et al., 2004). Furthermore, language and the appearance, style, gesture repertoire and attitude of the character can be tuned to each application's context, to user preferences, and more importantly to take into account cultural particularities.

The effects of animated characters on users and on the dynamics of user-system interaction are still unclear, as is the question of how to use them in order to maximize the benefits desired. However, the literature does report significant improvements in users' *perception* of the system and their interaction with it when the interface includes an animated character (Moundridou and Virvou, 2001; Mori et al., 2003; Van Mulken et al., 1998).

Proceedings of the Workshop on Embodied Language Processing, pages 33–40,
Prague, Czech Republic, June 28, 2007.

In what way and to what extent are the perceptions of users affected by the presence of an animated character in the system interface? And how does this affect users' opinion and acceptance of a biometric authentication system? We designed an experiment to learn a bit more about these important usability questions. Expanding on previous studies of factors that impact on the usability of a biometric authentication system, the present paper reports the differences we have found in the subjective perceptions of users interacting with our biometric authentication system through interfaces offering two different forms of assistance: information and assistance in the form of text shown on-screen, and given by a talking animated character.

In the following section we review a variety of social and user perception parameters identified in the literature as being potentially affected by an ECA. In section 3 we describe our user test framework and we show our results in section 4.

2 Background

According to Nass et al. (1994) human–machine interaction is fundamentally social. This has clear implications for user interface design. The user's view of how the system works doesn't always correspond to the actual way the technology works, but, rather, it depends on the user's preconceptions, on the interaction process itself and on mental models that are influenced by the system interface. Introducing an ECA in the interface can have a visual impact on the user that can affect her perception of the system as a whole. Ruttkay et al. (2002) compile a number of user parameters (such as trust, ease of use, effectiveness, and personal taste) that have been shown in the literature to be affected by the presence of an ECA.

Basically, there are two lines of work related to the effects of ECAs on the users' perception of a system. On one hand, the so called "persona effect," associated with the presence of the ECA, and on the other, effects connected with the characteristics or qualities a specific ECA might have.

2.1 The persona effect

People seem to like and enjoy using systems with ECAs more than without them, they tend to find systems easier to use and tasks easier to accomplish, and they also feel more motivated and find learning easier (both learning to use the system and learning about a particular subject in the case of teaching applications), even though their performance is in fact roughly the same as that of users interacting without the ECA: Some authors speculate that objective performance improvements beyond user perceptions will be achieved in the long-run. For instance, Moundridou and Virvou (2001) believe that the increased motivation of students using a tutor application with an animated character may enhance their learning capacity in the long-term.

Animated characters can even help contain user stress and frustration caused by difficulties during interaction with the system (Mori et al., 2003), and as a result they may improve the efficiency of the interaction over that of a text-only system (Hone et al., 2003). An interesting point is that many of these psychological effects are observed as a response to the mere presence of the animated character, without it providing any obvious cues or expression to help the user: people's perceptions have also been found to be affected by an ECA's behaviour. The phenomenon has been called 'Persona Effect' (Lester et al., 1997). Later research (Van Mulken et al., 1998) has shown that the mere presence of an ECA can make tasks seem easier and more enjoyable to the user. Furthermore, an ECA showing greater empathic emotion towards the user improves the latter's overall impression of the system and perception of ease of use (Brave et al., 2005; Mori et al., 2003).

The presence of a human-like character can also have potential dangers such as the system anthropomorphisation effect that may lead to users having unrealistic expectations that are frustrated by actual interaction, as Walker et al. (1994) points out, concluding that a human face in an interface can help attract the user's attention and increase her level of motivation. At the same time, however, it can create high expectations about the intelligence of the system, which can lead to frustration if they are then not met.

2.2 ECA feature-related effects

Some authors have studied how the *attitude* displayed by the ECA, for instance regarding its proactivity and reactivity (Xiao et. al, 2004), may induce in the user certain responses such as a sense of ease of use, system usefulness, frustration or sluggishness in task execution. Indeed, it has been shown that an affective and empathic attitude on the part of the ECA can have a very positive effect on the user's perception of the interaction, lowering the level of frustration (Hone et al., 2003; Mori et al., 2003) and improving the user's opinion of the system (Brave et. al 2005).

Another line of research deals with the *gestures* and nonverbal behaviour of the ECA. A good gestural repertoire may promote in the user a perception of naturalness of interaction with the system and system socialness (see, *e.g.*, Cassell and Bickmore, 2000).

The physical appearance of the ECA has also been seen to have an influence on the user. For instance, Leenheer (2006) has studied the effect of the colour of the clothing on the ECA, and Hone (2006) shows that a female character reduces user frustration levels better than a male one. Hone also points out that the actual efficiency of the interaction may depend on the ECAs characteristics.

Dehn and Van Mulken (2000) suggest that the great variability of results in the literature may be due not only to the different features of the ECAs across the studies, but also to the different areas of application in which the ECAs were used. In this paper we present a study of the influence of an ECA in a specific application domain: biometric authentication. First we identify the user perception parameters that we have considered may be affected by the ECA. Then we describe our exploratory test to examine the persona effect. We have left the observation of the effects of the physical, attitudinal and gestural features of the ECA for future experiments.

3 Test design

We created a multibiometric authentication test platform with two user interfaces, one with an ECA guiding the user through the steps of the required tasks, the other with the same information provided only through text displayed on the screen. We asked the users to carry out two general tasks: a) to try to access the system acting as impostors, and b) to enrol using their own biometric traits and then authenticate their real identity.

3.1 System architecture

The test platform architecture simulates a scenario in which a user has to securely access restricted information stored on a remote server across an IP network (Internet or Intranet). In order to access such information the user's identity must be authenticated on the basis of two biometric traits (hence our characterisation of the system as multibiometric). The user may choose the two modes she wishes to authenticate her identity with from among the following four: fingerprint, signature, voice and iris pattern.

The specific technologies used for each biometric mode were:

- Fingerprint: *Sensor:* Precise 100 digital fingerprint reader. *Software:* 'Precise Java' by Precise Biometrics. (Precise Biometrics, 2007).
- Signature: Sensor: Wacom Intuous2 A6 digitizing tablet (WACOM, 2007). *Software:* CiC iSign verification software (CIC, 2007).
- Voice: *Sensor:* standard microphone. *Software:* speech and speaker recognition by Nuance Communications (Nuance, 2007).
- Iris: *Sensor:* Panasonic Autenticam BM-100ET iris video camera (Panasonic, 2007). *Software:* 'Private ID' recognition algorithms by Iridian (Iridian Technologies, 2007).

3.2 User interface

We have created a web interface (using Java Applet technology) with five flaps; one to access the general instructions of use, and one for each of the four biometric modes (in left to right order: fingerprint, signature, voice and iris). Below is a biometric trait visualisation area and a text message bar through which (in addition to the ECA) the system guides the user throughout the interaction.

In addition, we divided the test users into two groups to which we presented two different interaction "metaphors":

- *ECA Metaphor:* An ECA is permanently present on the right side of the screen to assist the user by giving her general instructions and guiding her through the steps of the interaction. The ECA gives no information regarding the details of each particular biometric mode. The ECA has been created and integrated into our application using the technology provided by Haptek (Haptek, 2007). The ECA uses free Spanish Text-To-Speech (TTS) software (Lernout and Hauspie, 2007) to speak to the user. Figure 1 shows the interface with the ECA.

- *TEXT Metaphor*: The user is only guided through text messages.

Note: In the ECA metaphor the text message bar remains active, serving as subtitles to what the ECA says. The messages read by the ECA are exactly the same as those given in text form in both metaphores.

Figure 1: User interface for the multibiometric authentication system.

3.3 Description of the tests

We designed the tests following the recommendations issued by the International Biometric Group (IBG, 2006). We worked with a sample of 20 users, half of which interacted with the ECA metaphor and the other half with the TEXT metaphor. The users carried out the following tasks distributed in two separate sessions (on different days):

- On the first day an experimenter trained each participant in the use of each biometric mode. The training is specific for each mode and results in the creation of a biometric trait pattern for each user. After creating the user models the impostor tests were carried out. We allowed the users to consult the biometric traits (*i.e.*, fingerprint, signature, voice sample and picture of the iris) of four people (2 females and 2 males), and we asked them to choose one of them in each of five impersonation attempts. In order to access the system (in this case as impostors) users had to successfully mimic any two biometric traits of the same person. The system returned the result of the attempt (success or failure) at the end of the verification process. After taking all of the 5 attempts the users were directed to a web questionnaire to rate the ease of use, sense of security and preference of each of the biometric modes, and to give an overall score for the system.
- The second day the users were asked to authenticate their own identity. The task was to successfully access the system three times in a maximum of 6 attempts. Just as in the impostor attempts, users had to enter two of their biometric traits in succession, after which they were informed of the system's decision to accept or reject them. In case of failure in either of the two chosen modes, the system didn't inform the users of which mode failed. At the end of this second session the users completed another web questionnaire to give us their evaluation of system privacy and an overall score of merit for the system, and for each biometric mode they rated pleasantness, ease of use and preference. In addition, those users who interacted with the ECA metaphor were asked to rate the usefulness and pleasantness of the ECA.

In addition to the questionnaire information we collected user-system interaction efficiency data such as number of failures, verification times and so on. However, in this paper we focus primarily on the users' impressions. To summarise, the parameters we have analysed are Preference, Security, Ease-of-use, Pleasantness and Privacy, all measured on 7-point Likert scales.

4 Results

We carried out a series of two sample t-tests on the two groups of users (ECA Metaphor and TEXT Metaphor) and examined the influence of the ECA on the subjective parameters of the interaction. For each of the tests we propose a null hypothesis, H_O, and an alternative hypothesis, H_1. We have chosen the 5% (p=0.05) significance level to reject the null hypothesis. (The questionnaire values were normalised to values between –3 and 3 for statistical processing.)

4.1 Comparative analysis of the ECA y TEXT metaphors

Our general working hypothesis is that interaction with the ECA interface will be more pleasant for the user, which will result in a higher opinion of the system. We specify this in a series of hypotheses for each of the perception parameters we introduced in the previous section:

***Hypothesis 1*:**

H_O: ECA and TEXT Metaphor users rate the **ease-of-use** of the biometric modes equally.

H_1: ECA Metaphor users rate the **ease-of-use** of the biometric modes significantly **higher** than TEXT Metaphor users.

The average ease-of-use score for the ECA Metaphor is: μ_{ECA} = 1,30; and for the TEXT Metaphor: μ_{TEXT} = 0.65. The two sample t-test showed that the difference was statistically significant ($t(74)=1.94$; $p=0.028$). Therefore we may accept the alternative hypothesis that the ECA increases the user's perception of ease-of-use of biometric technology.

***Hypothesis 2*:**

H_O: ECA and TEXT Metaphor users rate the **pleasantness** of the biometric modes equally.

H_1: ECA Metaphor users rate the **pleasantness** of the biometric modes significantly **higher** than TEXT Metaphor users.

The average pleasantness score for the ECA Metaphor is: μ_{ECA} = 1.98; and for the TEXT Metaphor: μ_{TEXT} = 1.20; The two sample t-test showed that the difference was statistically significant ($t(77)=2.32$; $p=0.011$). Therefore we may accept the alternative hypothesis that the ECA increases the pleasantness of the interaction with the biometric modes.

***Hypothesis 3*:**

H_O: ECA and TEXT Metaphor users rate the **privacy** of the system equally.

H_1: ECA Metaphor users rate the **privacy** of the system significantly **higher** than TEXT Metaphor users.

The two sample t-test showed no statistically significant difference. We are therefore unable to reject the null hypothesis. Instead we propose the opposite alternative hypothesis:

***Hypothesis 3.1*:**

H_1: ECA Metaphor users rate the **privacy** of the system significantly **higher** than TEXT Metaphor users.

The average score for the perception of privacy for the ECA Metaphor is μ_{ECA}=-1.20; and for the TEXT Metaphor: μ_{TEXT}=-0.60. The two sample t-test showed that the difference was statistically significant ($t(67)=-3.42$; $p=0.001$). Thus we accept in this case the alternative hypothesis that users' perception of privacy is lower with the ECA Metaphor than with the TEXT Metaphor. This result might lend support to Zajonc's (1965) suggestion that the presence of a character may enhance arousal or user sensitivity, which might explain why the user might feel uneasy letting the agent have her personal biometric traits.

***Hypothesis 4*:**

H_O: ECA and TEXT Metaphor users rate their perception of **security** of the biometric modes equally.

H_1: ECA Metaphor users' trust in the **security** of the biometric modes is **higher** than in the case of the TEXT Metaphor users.

We obtained no statistically significant results, so we reverse the alternative hypothesis:

***Hypothesis 4.1*:**

H_1: ECA Metaphor users' trust in the **security** of the biometric modes is **lower** than in the case of the TEXT Metaphor users.

Once more, our results were not statistically significant. Therefore we cannot infer any relationship between the presence of an ECA and users' sense security of a biometric system.

***Hypothesis 5*:**

H_O: Interaction with the ECA Metaphor and with the TEXT Metaphor is equally **efficient**.

H_1: Interaction with the ECA Metaphor is **more efficient** that interaction with the TEXT Metaphor.

The objective parameter categories compared were speed (verification times and reaction times) and efficiency (number of verification failures, false matches and false rejections). We found no statistically significant differences between the averages of any of these variables across the two metaphors. Therefore we cannot determine any influence of the ECA on the actual efficiency of the interaction.

The fact that our system is multibiometric –in that it requires simultaneous verification of two from among four possible biometric traits– affects the complexity of the verification process (Ubuek, 2003). We now look at the effect our ECA had on the users' perception of the cognitive demand and of the need for the extra security our multibiometric system is supposed to provide:

***Hypothesis 6*:**

H_O: ECA and TEXT Metaphor users feel equally about the need to require two biometric modes for identity verification to ensure **security**.

H_1: ECA Metaphor users feel that the requirement of two biometric modes for verification enhances **security** to a **greater** extent than in the case of the TEXT Metaphor users.

The average score for the perceived need for the enhanced security provided by multibiometrics is, for the ECA Metaphor: μ_{ECA}= 2.8; and for the TEXT Metaphor: μ_{TEXT}=2.1. The two sample t-test showed that the difference was statistically significant ($t(12)=2.28$; $p=0.021$). Therefore we may confirm the alternative hypothesis.

We found no statistically significant differences between the two metaphors regarding the users' perception of the extra cognitive demand of multibiometrics.

Table 1 summarises our results.

EFFECTS ON THE USER	ECA Metaphor (vs. TEXT Metaphor)
Subjective impressions of users	Greater ease-of-use Greater pleasantness
	Less privacy
User behaviour throughout the interaction with the system	We didn't reach definitive conclusions
Improvement in task execution	We didn't reach definitive conclusions
Impressions regarding multibiometrics	Enhanced security

Table 1: Comparative results

5 Conclusions and future lines of research

Some of the most serious obstacles to widespread use that biometic technology is facing are related to user interaction and acceptance. We believe the results presented in this paper open interesting new lines of research. We found that the presence of an ECA (persona effect) makes users experience interaction as easier and more pleasant. Regarding sense of security, our results are in line with other studies on ECAs. The increased pleasantness of use of the biometric modes could help overcome users' reluctance to accept biometric systems. On the other hand, the presence of the ECA could have a negative affect by enhancing the users' perception of encroachment on their privacy.

We believe it may be possible to increase the level of users' perceived privacy and user trust by adopting strategies such as allowing the user to personalise the appearance and even the behaviour of the avatar, as Xiao et al. (2007) suggest. Giving the ECA greater and more natural communication skills (e.g., small talk, specific gestures, etc.) and a more empathic attitude (in line with ideas in the area of affective computing) could have further positive effects.

We may mention the inclusion of ECAs on multibiometric systems as another interesting specific line of research, given the enhancement in the users' perception of the security of such systems compared to the same without ECA.

6 Acknowledgements

This study has been possible thanks to the support grant received from the TEC2006-13170-C02-02 project of the Spanish Plan Nacional de I+D and the 04-AEC0620-000046/06 ("Recognition of facial and speech patterns for safe multimodal services in mobile communications") project by Telefónica, funded by the Comunidad Autonoma de Madrid.

7 References

Jonas Beskow, Inger Karlsson, Jo Kewley and Giampiero Salvi, 2004. *SYNFACE - A Talking Head Telephone for the Hearing-impaired.* In Computers helping people with special needs 1178-1186.

Biosec: Biometry and Security, 2004. *Deliverable D6.3: Report on results of first phase usability testing and guidelines for developers.* Available at: http://www.europeanbiometrics.info/images/resources/73_471_file.pdf (Accessed: 2007, March)

Scott Brave, Clifford Nass, and Kevin Hutchinson, 2005. *Computers that care: investigating the effects of orientation of emotion exhibited by an embodied computer agent*. In International Journal of Human Computer Studies, vol. 62, pp. 161-178.

Justine Cassell and Tim Bickmore, 2000. *External manifestations of trustworthiness in the interface*. In Communications of the ACM, vol. 43, pp. 50-56.

CIC, 2007. Communication Intelligence Corporation, "iSign for Java," http://www.cic.com/products/isign/#iSignJava (Accessed: 2007, March)

Doris M. Dehn and Sussane Van Mulken, 2000. *The impact of animated interface agents: a review of empirical research*. In International Journal of Human-Computer Studies, vol. 52, pp. 1-22.

Haptek, 2007. http://www.haptek.com (Accessed: 2007, March)

Kate Hone, Farah Akhtar and Martin Saffu, 2003. *Affective agents to reduce user frustration: the role of agent embodiment*. In Proceedings of Human-Computer Interaction (HCI2003), Bath, UK, 2003.

Kate Hone, 2006. *Empathic agents to reduce user frustration: The effects of varying agent characteristics*. In Interacting with Computers, vol. 18, pp. 227-245.

Matt Huenerfauth, 2005. *American Sign Language Generation: Multimodal NLG with Multiple Linguistic Channels*. In Proceedings of the ACL Student Research Workshop (ACL 2005), pp. 37–42.

IBG, 2006. International Biometric Group, 2006. Comparative Biometric Testing Available at: http://www.biometricgroup.com/reports/public/comparative_biometric_testing.html (Accessed: 2007, March)

Iridian Technologies, 2007. Private ID. http://www.iridiantech.com/products.php?page=1 (Accessed: 2007, March)

Rinze Leenheer, 2006. *Should ECAs 'dress to impress'?*, 4th Twente Student Conference on IT, 2006.

James C. Lester, Sharolyn A. Converse, Susan E. Kahler, S. Todd Barlow, Brian A. Stone, and Ravinder S. Bhogal, 1997. *The persona effect: affective impact of animated pedagogical agents*.In Proceedings of the SIGCHI conference on Human factors in computing systems, pp. 359-366.

Lernout and Hauspie, 2007. http://www.microsoft.com/msagent/downloads/user.asp (Accessed: 2007, March)

Junichiro Mori, Helmut Prendinger and Mitsuru Ishizuka, 2003. *Evaluation of an Embodied Conversational Agent with Affective Behavior*. In Proceedings of the AAMAS03 Workshop on Embodied Conversational Characters as Individuals , Melbourne, Australia.

Maria Moundridou and Maria Virvou, 2001. *Evaluating the Impact of Interface Agents in an Intelligent Tutoring Systems Authoring Tool*. In Proceedings of the Panhellenic Conference with International participation in Human-Computer interaction.

Clifford Nass, Jonathan Steuer, and Ellen R. Tauber, 1994. *Computers are social actors*. In Proceedings of the SIGCHI Conference on Human Factors in Computing Systems: Celebrating interdependence. CHI '94. ACM Press, New York, NY, 72-78.

Nuance, 2007. Nuance Communications Inc. http://www.nuance.com (Accessed: 2007, March)

Panasonic, 2007. http://www.panasonic.com (Accessed: 2007, March)

Precise Biometrics, 2007. http://www.precisebiometrics.com/ (Accessed: 2007, March)

Zsófia Ruttkay, Claire Dormann and Han Noot, 2002. *Evaluating ECAs - What and How?*. In Proceedings of AAMAS 2002 Workshop on Embodied Conversational Agents -- Let's Specify and Evaluate Them!, Bologna, Italy.

Angela Sasse, 2004. *Usability and trust in information systems*. Cyber Trust & Crime Prevention Project. University College London.

Susanne Van Mulken, Elisabeth Andre, and Jochen Muller, 1998. *The Persona Effect: How substantial is it?*. In Proceedings of the ACM CHI 1998 Conference , pp. 53-66. Los Angeles, CA

WACOM, 2007. http://www.wacom.com (Accessed: 2007, March)

Janet H. Walker, Lee Sproull and R. Subramani, 1994. *Using a human face in an interface*. In Proceedings of the SIGCHI conference on Human factors in computing systems: celebrating interdependence, pp. 85-91.

James Wayman, Anil K. Jain, Davide Maltoni and Maio Daio, 2005. Biometric Systems: Technology, Design and Performance Evaluation, *Springer*.

Jun Xiao, John Stasko and Richard Catrambone, 2004. *An Empirical Study of the Effect of Agent Competence on User Performance and Perception*. In Proceedings of the Third International Joint Conference on Autonomous Agents and Multiagent Systems-Volume 1, pp. 178-185.

Jun Xiao, John Stasko and Richard Catrambone, 2007. *The Role of Choice and Customization on Users' In-*

teraction with Embodied Conversational Agents: Effects on Perception and Performance, Proceedings of CHI 2007, San Jose, CA.

Robert B. Zajonc, 1965. *Social Facilitation*, Science, 149, pp. 269-274.

Coordination in Conversation and Rapport

Justine Cassell, Alastair J. Gill and Paul A. Tepper
Center for Technology & Social Behavior
Northwestern University
2240 Campus Drive, Evanston, IL 60208
{justine, alastair, ptepper}@northwestern.edu

Abstract

We investigate the role of increasing friendship in dialogue, and propose a first step towards a computational model of the role of long-term relationships in language use between humans and embodied conversational agents. Data came from a study of friends and strangers, who either could or could not see one another, and who were asked to give directions to one-another, three subsequent times. Analysis focused on differences in the use of dialogue acts and non-verbal behaviors, as well as co-occurrences of dialogue acts, eye gaze and head nods, and found a pattern of verbal and nonverbal behavior that differentiates the dialogue of friends from that of strangers, and differentiates early acquaintances from those who have worked together before. Based on these results, we present a model of deepening rapport which would enable an ECA to begin to model patterns of human relationships.

1 Introduction

What characterizes the language of people who have known one another for a long time? In the US one thinks of groups of friends, leaning in towards one another, laughing, telling jokes at one another's expense, and interrupting one another in their eagerness to contribute to the conversation. The details may differ from culture to culture, but the fact of differences between groups of friends and groups of strangers are probably universal. Which characteristics, if any, reliably differentiates friends and strangers? Which can make a new friend feel welcome? An old friend feel appreciated? Advances in natural language are ensuring that embodied conversational agents (ECAs) are increasingly scintillating, emotionally and socially expressive, and personality-rich. However, for the most part, those same ECAs demonstrate amnesia, beginning every conversation with a user as if it is their first, and never getting past the stage of introductory remarks.

As the field of ECAs matures, and these systems are found on an increasing number of platforms, for an increasing number of applications, we feel that it is time to ensure that ECAs be able to engage in deepening relationships that make their collaboration with humans productive and satisfying over long periods of time. To this end, in this paper we examine the verbal and nonverbal correlates of friendship in an empirical study, and then take first steps towards a model of deepening friendship and rapport in ECAs. The current study is a part of a larger research program into linguistic and social coordination devices from the utterance level to the relationship level – how they work in humans, how they can be modeled in virtual humans, and how virtual humans can be used to teach people who wish to learn these skills.

2 Background & Theory

As people become closer, their conversational style changes. They may raise more topics in the course of a conversation, refer more to themselves as a single unit than as two people, and be more responsive to one another's talk (Cassell & Tversky, 2005; Hornstein, 1982). They also are likely to sustain eye contact longer, smile more, and lean more towards one another (Grahe & Bernieri, 1999; Richmond & McCroskey, 1995). In addition, friends appear to have fewer difficulties with lexical search, perhaps because they can rely on greater shared knowledge, and are more likely to talk at the same time, and to negotiate turn-taking in a less rigid manner, both through gaze and ges-

Proceedings of the Workshop on Embodied Language Processing, pages 41–50,
Prague, Czech Republic, June 28, 2007.

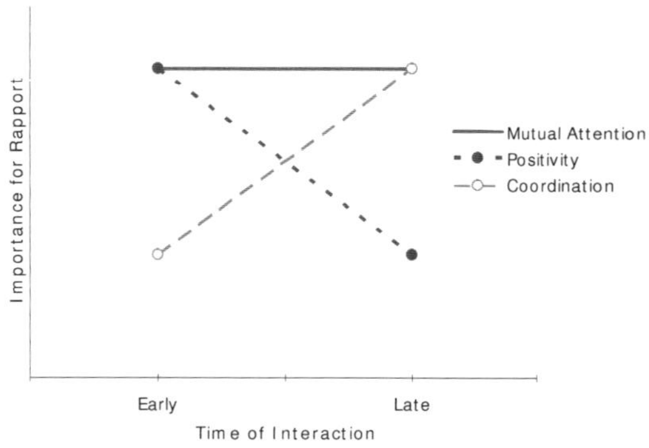

Figure 1. Three component model of rapport (from Tickle-Degen & Rosenthal, 1990).

ture (Welji & Duncan, 2005). Tickle-Degnen & Rosenthal (1990) propose a model of deepening rapport over time based on the relationship among three components: positivity, mutual attention and coordination. As shown in Figure 1, as friendship deepens, the importance of positivity decreases, while the importance of coordination increases. Attention to the conversational partner, however, is hypothesized to remain constant. That is, strangers are more likely to be polite and uniformly positive in their talk, but also more likely to be awkward and badly coordinated with their interlocutors.

As a relationship progresses and impressions have been formed and accepted, disagreement becomes acceptable and important. This may entail an increase in face-threatening issues and behaviors (cf. Brown & Levinson, 1987) accompanied by a decrease in the need to mediate these threats. At this stage in the relationship, coordination becomes highly important, so that the conversation will be less awkward and there is less likelihood of misunderstanding. Attention to one another, however, does not change. Tickle-Degnen & Rosenthal point out that these features are as likely to be expressed nonverbally (through smiles, nods, and posture shifts, for example) as verbally.

One criticism of Tickle-Degnen & Rosenthal, and similar work, is that positive feelings for, and knowledge about, the other person are not distinguished (Cappella, 1990). That is, what might be perceived as lack of rapport could actually be a lack of familiarity with a partner's behavioral cues for indicating misunderstanding or requesting information.

This conflation may come from the fact that the word rapport is used both to refer to the phenomenon of instant responsiveness ("we just clicked") and that of deepening interdependence over time. ECA research has been divided between a focus on instant rapport (Gratch et al., 2006; Maatman, Gratch, & Marsella, 2005) and a focus on establishing and maintaining relationships over time (Bickmore & Picard, 2005; Cassell & Bickmore, 2002; Stronks, Nijholt, van der Vet, & Heylen, 2002). Perhaps due to difficulties with analyzing dyadic interdependent processes, and modeling them in computational systems, much of the work in both traditions still takes a *signaling* approach, whereby particular signals (such as nodding or small talk) demonstrate the responsiveness, extroversion, or rapport-readiness of the agent, but are decontextualized from the actions of the dyad (Duncan, 1990). Although this approach is well paired to current technological constraints, it may not adequately account for the contingency of interpersonal interaction and conversation. In addition, in none of these previous studies was there a focus on how verbal and nonverbal devices actually change over the course of a relationship, and how those devices are interdependent between speaker and listener. An instant rapport approach is useful for building systems that are initially attractive to users; but a system that signals increasing familiarity and intimacy through its linguistic and nonverbal behaviors may encourage users to stay with the system over a longer period of time.

In the current work, we concentrate how discourse and nonverbal behavior changes over time, and across the dyad, as this perspective allows us to highlight the similarities between interpersonal coordination and knowledge coordination of the kind that has been studied in both conversational analysis and psycholinguistics.

Work on conversational analysis demonstrates the importance of knowledge coordination components such as turn-taking and adjacency pairs (e.g.Goodwin, 1981; Schegloff & Sacks, 1973). Inspired by this approach, work by Clark and collaborators on grounding and conversation as joint action has made demonstrated coordination and cooperation as defining characteristics of conversation (Clark, 1996; Clark & Brennan, 1991; Clark & Wilkes-Gibbs, 1986). This work has in turn, received a significant amount of attention in computational linguistics, specifically in the study of dialogue (Matheson, Poesio, & Traum, 2000; Nakano, Reinstein, Stocky, & Cassell, 2003; Traum, 1994; Traum & Dillenbourg, 1998). To develop a model of nonverbal grounding, Nakano et al. (2003) studied people giving directions with respect to a map placed in between them. In that study, we observed that when a direction-receiver looked up from the map while the direction-giver was still giving directions, the giver would initiate grounding behavior such as a repeat or a rephrase.

The literature reviewed above leads us to believe that there is an integral relationship between social and knowledge coordination. In this paper, we attempt to draw conclusions about the changes in social and linguistic coordination over the short- and long-term in a way that illuminates that potential relationship, and that is also computationally viable. In order to do this, we replicate the task we used in our earlier grounding study (Nakano et al., 2003); that is we use a direction-giving task, where half the subjects can see one another, and half are divided by a screen. Here, however, half of the subjects in each visibility condition are friends and half are strangers. And to study the potential development of rapport across the experimental period, each pair performs three subsequent direction-giving tasks.

In the next section, we discuss the experimental procedure further. In section 4, we introduce first steps towards a new computational model of rapport that incorporates conversational coordination and grounding, based on our empirical findings.

3 The Experiment

3.1 Method

Participants We collected eight task-based conversations (N = 16): in each dyad, one participant was accompanied by the experimenter and followed a specific route from one place in the rococo university building where the experiment was run to another place in the building. S/he gave the other participant directions on how to reach that location, without the use of maps or other props. The direction-receiver (Receiver) was instructed to ask the direction-giver (Giver) as many questions as needed to understand the directions. After the conversation, the Receiver had to find the location. During recruitment the Giver was always selected as someone familiar with the building, while the Receiver was unfamiliar. All subjects were undergraduate students, and were motivated by surprise gifts hidden at the target location.

Design. We manipulated long-term rapport, visibility, and subsequent route in a $2 \times 2 \times 3$ design. We operationalized long-term rapport as a binary, between-subjects variable, with conditions Friends (self-reported as friends for at least one year) and Strangers. To study the effect of non-verbal behavior, we manipulated visibility as a second between-subject variable. To do this, half of the participants could see each other, and half were separated by a dividing panel. To study the effect of acquaintance across the experimental period, each dyad completed the task three consecutive times, going to three different locations.

Data Coding All dyads were videotaped using a six-camera array, capturing the participants' body movements from the front, side, and above, along with close-up views of their faces. From each dyad, we made time-aligned transcriptions (using Praat). Non-verbal behavior was coded using Anvil. From the transcripts, the following 9 DAMSL Dialogue Acts (Core & Allen, 1997) were coded: *Acknowledgments, Answers, Assert, Completion, Influence, Information Request, Reassert, Repeat-Rephrase,* and *Signal Non Understanding*. Non-verbal behavior in giver and receiver was coded using the following categories, based on Nakano, et al. (2003):

- *Look at Speaker* – looking at the speaker's eyes, eye region or face.
- *Look at Hearer* – looking at the hearer's eyes, eye region or face.
- *Head nod [speaker or hearer]* – Head moves up and down in a single continuous movement on a vertical axis, but eyes do not go above the horizontal axis.

3.2 Results

We first provide basic statistics on the experimental manipulations and then examine the role of friendship and visibility on verbal and non-verbal behavior.

Basic Statistics: Overall, we find that Friend dyads use a significantly greater number of turns per minute than Strangers ($t(6)= 2.45$, $p<.05$, two tail), however, there is no difference in the mean number of seconds it took for dyads to complete the task. This lack of significance may have been due to variance among the dyads, since the mean length was 847 seconds for friends and 1049 for

DV	Source	DF	DF Total	F Ratio
ACK	V*F	1	20	10.64**
COMP	V*F	1	4	9.78*
SNU	V*F	1	20	3.31†
	Rte	2	20	3.38*

Note: †p<0.08; *p < 0.05; **p < 0.01;

Table 1: Verbal behavior

Abbreviation: ACK=Acknowledgment; COMP=Completion; SNU=Signal Non Understanding; Sources abbreviated as: F = Friendship; V = Visibility; Rte = Route

strangers. Given the instructional nature of the task, this means that Friends were more likely to intervene in the direction-giving than were Strangers, even though – for most of the dyads – friends appear to take less time to finish. No difference was found in turns per minute for Visible and Non-visible dyads; nor is there a difference in length in seconds. For routes, there is no difference in turns per minute, however for the length of the route in seconds there is a difference ($F(2,21)=10.66$; $p<.006$) such that the mean length of Route 1 is 165 seconds; Route 2 is 395 seconds; Route 3 is 387. For this reason, all statistics below are normalized as a function of the length of that dyad's data in seconds, and graphs are plotted to show least squares mean.

Verbal and Nonverbal behavior: We examine the relationship between friendship and visibility of both Giver and Receiver across the three route tasks. Each of the DAMSL dialogue act variables and Non-verbal behavior variables was entered as the dependent variable in building mixed method models using the JMP statistical package (Version 6, SAS Institute Inc., Cary, NC, 1989-2005); Speaker (direction-giver or receiver), Visibility, Friendship and Route were entered as predictor variables; experimental dialogue number was also entered as a source of random variance. We report the results in Tables 1 and 2 (for DAMSL and Non-verbal behavior variables respectively).

Verbal Behavior: In terms of overall variance explained, we find that Acknowledgments is best accounted for by the model (Adjusted R Square of 0.91), whilst Completion is least well accounted for (Adjusted R^2 of 0.06).

Turning first to main effects, for Visibility, Visible-Givers use Acknowledgements, Assert, Influence, and Reassert dialogue acts more frequently than Non-visible Givers (post-hoc t tests at $p <.05$)

Visible-Receivers use Acknowledgement, Repeat-rephrase, Signal Non Understanding these features more frequently than Non-visible Receivers. (post-hoc t tests at $p <.05$)

For Friendship, no differences were found for production of DAMSL acts by givers. For receivers, receiver-strangers use more acknowledgements than receiver friends.

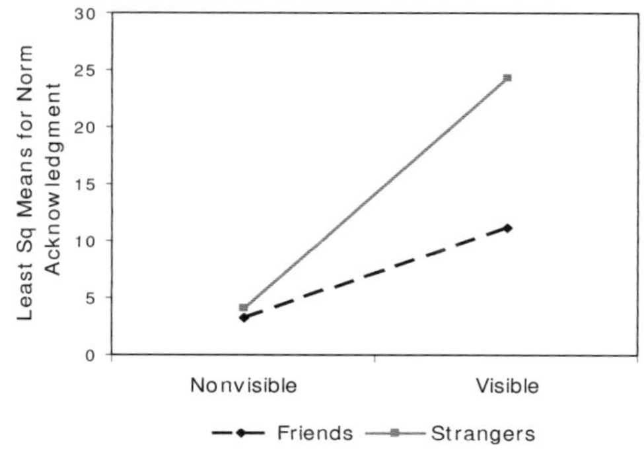

Figure 2: Giver Acknowledgment by condition

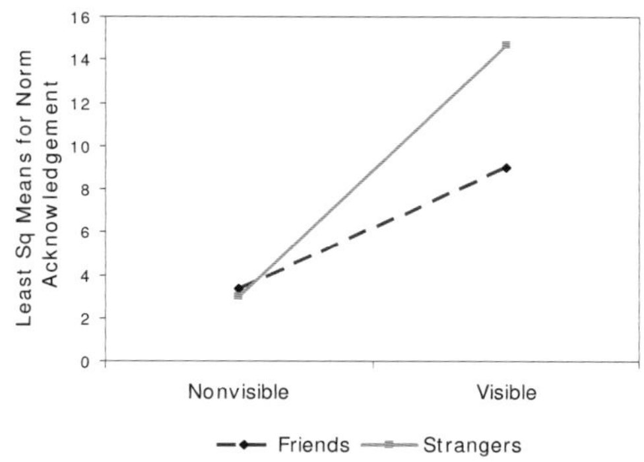

Figure 3: Receiver Acknowledgment by condition

These main effects are mediated by an interaction between VisibilityxFriendship for Acknowledgements. Here, as shown in Figure 2 and 3 we see that in the nonvisibility condition, there is no difference in the use of acknowledgements per second between friends and strangers; on the other hand, strangers use more acknowledgements in the visible condition ($p<.05$). A very similar interaction was found for Signal Non Understanding (at the trend level of $p<.08$).

Route is only a main effect predictor of Signal Non Understanding as used by receivers, who produce it significantly more frequently during the third route task than the first. Since signaling one's lack of understanding is potentially face-

DV	Source	DF	DF Total	F Ratio
Look At Speaker	Rte	2	10	18.03***
Hearer Nod	SPKR*F*Rte	2	20	5.14*
Speaker Nod	SPKR*F*Rte	2	20	4.21*

*p<0.05;**p<0.01; ***p<0.001

Table 2. Non Verbal Behaviors.

Sources abbreviated as: SPKR = Speaker; F = Friendship; V = Visibility; Rte = Route,

threatening, this result may indicate that both friends and strangers become more comfortable with one another by the third route.

Nonverbal Behavior: Variance explained by the non-verbal models is the greatest for Look At Speaker (Adjusted R^2 0.83) and least for Speaker Nod (0.38). With respect to the main effects resulting from the analysis of the non-verbal behaviors, we find the following.

Visibility: Givers nod more in the visible condition when the receiver is speaking than they do in the Non-visible condition.

Route: For both givers and receivers, there is an increase in use of Look At Speaker and Look At Hearer, over time; in both cases significantly greater instances of these variables occurred during Route task 2 and 3, compared to Route 1. Once again, these results may indicate increasing coordination in conversational behavior for both Friends and Strangers.

In fact, in the case of head nods, we note an interesting pattern of coordination between speaker and hearer head-nods across the routes that differs for friends and strangers. For friends, both Receiver and Giver head nods in response to Receiver talk reduce in frequency between the first and second routes (Giver $t(8)=-2.36$; $p<0.05$; Receiver $t(8)=-2.28$; $p<0.05$). For strangers, no such accommodation over time occurs. Conversely, for friends when the Giver is speaking, both giver and receiver head nods increase over the three routes (significant only for Receiver $t(8)=2.38$; $p<0.05$). For strangers, however, head nods decrease (Giver $t(8)=-2.80$; $p<0.05$, Receiver $t(8)=3.92$; $p<0.01$). This means that speaker and hearer are increasingly coordinated across the routes, particularly when they are friends.

Interaction of verbal and nonverbal behavior

So far we have concentrated on how individual verbal and nonverbal behaviors differ across conditions. However, this does not take account of the interactive nature of the task and the focus of this paper. We therefore examine how specific responsive nonverbal behaviors (looking at speaker/hearer and head nods) co-occur before, during, or after the DAMSL variables. Examination of the residuals of chi square analysis was used to identify co-occurrence of DAMSL dialogue acts with nonverbal behavior for each Speaker (Giver or Receiver) and condition (Friend/Stranger, Visible /Nonvisible). Significant over-use or underuse of these verbal/nonverbal co-occurrences was then compared using the log-likelihood statistic (Rayson, 2003) to dialogues in the other conditions (e.g., Giver-Friend-Visible with Giver-Friend-Nonvisible, and Giver-Stranger-Visible for Head-nods, and just Friends with Strangers for the Gaze data). This technique, which we used in our earlier grounding experiment (Nakano et al., 2003) allows us insight into the probable causality of the behaviors of speaker and hearer, across verbal and nonverbal behavior.

When direction-givers are speaking

Head-nods. Givers did not nod significantly more or less frequently across Friends/Strangers conditions when they were speaking.

Gaze. More than in friendship dialogues, when strangers are speaking, and the direction-giver is acknowledging, the direction-receiver is likely to look at the Giver ($G^2=17.14$; $p<0.0001$).

More than in friendship dialogues, in Stranger dialogues, both before and after the direction-giver asserts something, the Receiver is likely to look at the Giver ($G^2=5.09$; $p<0.05$, and $G^2=4.16$, $p<0.05$, respectively).

More than in friendship dialogues, both before and during the Giver's use of Repeat-Rephrase utterances, the Receiver is likely to look at the Giver ($G^2=35.02$; $p<0.0001$, and $G^2=60.74$; $p<0.0001$, respectively).

More than in friendship dialogues, both before and during the Giver's use of Info-Request dialogue acts, the Receiver is likely to look at the Giver ($G^2=39.01$; $p<0.0001$, and $G^2=9.60$; $p<0.01$, respectively).

This means that right after a direction receiver looks at the direction-giver, the giver produces an Assertion, a Repeat-Rephrase, or an Information

Request. As with Nakano et al., the stranger's gaze towards the direction-giver can be seen as a signal of non-understanding and, in these contexts, it evokes one of these three grounding responses from the direction-giver.

For friends, on the other hand, gaze towards the speaker evokes the next segment of the directions, and is therefore functioning as a signal of understanding. That is, more than in stranger dialogues, both before and during the Giver's use of Influence dialogue acts (utterances such as "turn right"), Receivers are more to look at the Giver (G^2=4.77; p<0.05, and G^2=31.92; p<0.0001, respectively).

When direction-receivers are speaking

Head-nods. As shown in Figure 4, Strangers used more head nods than Friends during their use of Acknowledgment dialogue acts in the visible condition (G^2 = 10.48, p<.01), however they do not differ from friends in the nonvisible condition (G^2 = 0.01, *ns*).

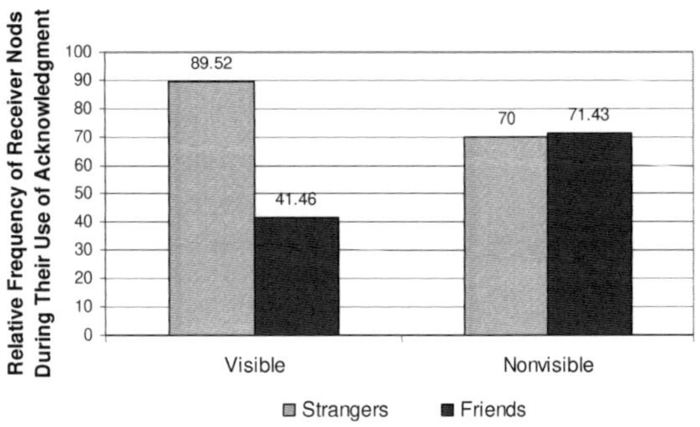

Figure 4: Receiver nods during Acknowledgment

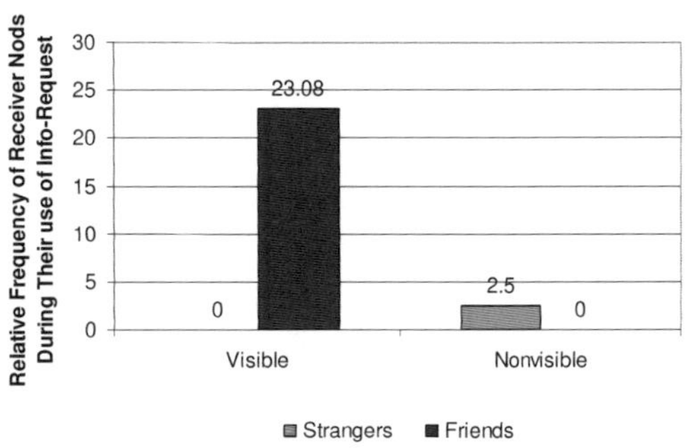

Figure 5: Receiver nods during Info Request

Conversely, as shown in Figure 5, when receivers are making an Info-Request in the visible condition (G^2=14.13, p<.001), Friends nod much more often than Strangers; but do not differ from Strangers in the nonvisible condition (G^2 = 1.44, *ns*). Once again, here the friends are marking their understanding, by nodding, even while they request further information.

Gaze. Before the Receiver's use of Acknowledgment dialogue acts in Stranger dialogues, the Giver is more likely to look at the Receiver (G^2=10.79; p<0.01). After the Receiver has used an Acknowledgment in a Stranger dialogue, s/he is more likely to look at the Giver a (G^2=14.79; p<0.001). This means that among strangers the giver and receiver are likely to engage in mutual gaze around the acknowledgement dialogue act.

During and after a Repeat-Rephrase dialogue act in Friends dialogues, the Receiver is more likely to look at the Giver (G^2=10.37; p<0.01 and G^2=6.72; p<0.01, respectively). Before the Receiver uses a Repeat-Rephrase dialogue act in a Friends dialogues, the Giver is more likely to look at the Receiver (G^2=9.08; p<0.01). This means that among friends, giver and receiver engage in mutual gaze around the repeat and rephrase dialogue act.

3.3 Discussion

Our analysis of verbal and non-verbal behaviors reveals consistent differences across the short term, comparing subsequent direction-giving tasks, and across the long term, comparing strangers to friends.

Strangers – Knowledge coordination

With respect to the co-ordination of verbal and nonverbal behavior, it is apparent that, among strangers, the Receiver's use of Acknowledgments is strongly associated with characteristic gaze patterns of signaling non-understanding. In these Stranger dyads, the Giver looks at the Receiver to signal the need for feedback. The Receiver then nods to emphasize comprehension while uttering the Acknowledgment (e.g., "okay"), and then looks back at the Giver. This pattern is very specific to Strangers, and in the case of the Receiver's use of head nod, specific to the visible condition. Similarly, among strangers, when the Giver acknowledges the receiver's correct understanding, the Receiver looks at the Giver. This pattern of gaze request, and grounding response, happens repeatedly and often (Acknowledgements being used more frequently by strangers), ensuring coordination among strangers, but at the cost of frequent explicit requests. Of course, since Acknowledgements are generally backchannel utterances, used to indicate mutual understanding, one explanation for the higher frequency of acknowledgements, head nods and eye gaze by strangers, especially in the earlier tasks, is over-generation aimed at showing attention. Although over-generation could achieve these goals, it can also result in creating a false impression of mutual understanding and it is notable that these behaviors decrease over time.

We also find that in the Strangers condition, Receivers are more likely to look at the Giver before and during the Giver's use of Repeat-Rephrase (i.e., repeating back to the Receiver some earlier information), and also before and during the Giver's use of Info-Request acts (that is the Giver asking the Receiver a question such as "do you get that?").

From the frequent and repeated use of Acknowledgments and gaze (implying something like "okay... are you sure you're okay... really?"), to the Receiver's gaze-anticipation of the Giver's Repeat-Rephrase and Info-Request, we infer a much more effortful interaction for Strangers, and one that, in fact, for most dyads, takes longer.

In line with Welji and Duncan (2005), we found evidence that the task may demand additional cognitive resources for Strangers, with the Receiver in the Strangers dialogues breaking gaze at the Giver to apparently consult some internal representation of the space just described by the Givers Assert (e.g., "you'll find some blue couches"), before returning attention, and gaze, once again to the Giver.

We also note a greater use overall of Acknowledgment and Completions by Strangers and in visible situations; Receivers in the visible situations also use more Signal Non Understanding. Taken together, these findings indicate that coordination and achieving mutual understanding is more effortful for Strangers: Friends use fewer dialogue acts such as Acknowledgment, Completion, and Signal Non Understanding, indicating that there is less need to negotiate understanding, and that they are more likely to have some kind of shared representation. Because of this, the Friends dialogues and task performance would appear to be more efficient, with less grounding required and less mutual gaze around their use of Acknowledgments, Info-Requests and Repeat-Rephrase.

The fact that Friends are better able to calibrate the task than Strangers is also demonstrated by the results found for Route. Both Friend and Stranger dyads increase their gaze towards one another from Route 1 to Route 2. But Friends shift the way they use head nods over the course of the three routes. They begin in Route 1 by producing them in conjunction with Receiver talk (acknowledgment, request for further information, repeating directions back). However, by Route 2, the friends are nodding when the direction-giver speaks, marking that they don't need further information but have understood on the first try. On the contrary, Strangers continue to nod just as much with receiver talk, and decrease their nods with giver talk; perhaps since by Route 2, it is clear that Strangers don't understand on the first try.

Tickle-Degnen and Rosenthal (1990) predict greater coordination as a relationship progresses. We found better coordination, but that was revealed, paradoxically, through fewer coordination devices and fewer dialogue acts in each turn, both comparing from Route 1 to Route 3, and comparing Strangers to Friends.

Friends – Positivity

In the Friends dialogues, we find a notable collocation of non-verbal behavior and the Receiver's use of Repeat-Rephrase utterance (i.e., repeating the Giver's utterance back to ensure correct interpretation). This is in contrast to the findings for Stranger dyads which found nonverbal behaviors found in conjunction with the Giver's reactive use of Repeat-Rephrase – i.e., the Giver's questioning of the Receiver's understanding – perhaps after a breakdown in mutual understanding. In the Friend dyads, it is the Receiver who proactively checks correct understanding of the Giver's utterance before the interaction continues.

Tickle-Degnen & Rosenthal predict a reduction in the importance of positivity as rapport increases over time in a relationship. We found some evidence to support this, since such questioning of the Giver in itself may be viewed as face-threatening behavior. However, in the Friends dialogues, this Repeat-Rephrase appears anticipated – or sanctioned – by the Giver who looks at the Receiver prior to the utterance. Further, during and after the Receivers' use of the Repeat-Rephrase utterance, they also look at the Giver, which again would be expected to be viewed as a threat to face.

Similarly, the Receiver gazes at the Giver before and during the Giver's use of Influence dialogue acts (explicit commands, such as "turn left"). Such direct gaze, along with a reduced number of mediating dialogue acts such as Acknowledgments, appears to indicate that Friends dialogues are less concerned with avoiding face-threatening behavior, and as such would appear less concerned with maintaining positivity during the interaction.

Note that, almost paradoxically, Friends demonstrate their increased ability to coordinate their interaction through a diminished use of explicit coordination devices. This speeds up the interaction, and reduces the number of overall dialogue acts.

And, finally, differences between Friends and Strangers are vastly diminished when the interlocutors cannot see one another. This leads us to believe that nonverbal behaviors in addition to gaze and head nods may be playing a role in how Friends coordinate with one another; an advantage which is taken away when they can only hear one another's voices.

4 Towards a Computational Model

In the short-term context of conversation, maintenance of mutual attention and incremental coordination of beliefs are requisites for grounding and turn-taking. In prior computational systems, grounding has been achieved by marking the status of conversational contributions as provisional (ungrounded) or shared (grounded). Conversational actions by either the user or the system can trigger updates that change provisional information to shared. Acknowledgements, for example, are explicit ways of achieving grounding, but moving on to the next stage of the task is equally effective, as it presupposes that prior utterances have been taken up (Traum, 1994). In a model such as this, grounding occurs at the turn level. In order to handle the multimodal phenomena that participate in grounding in face-to-face conversation, as Nakano et al. (Nakano et al., 2003) have shown, a model of knowledge coordination needs to have more frequently updated access to potential grounding events. In that implementation, we continuously polled for inputs, so as to capture the updates in grounding that occur between typical linguistic segments. We believe that the focus on time and process that allowed us to look at events of a smaller granularity in our earlier work on nonverbal grounding behavior will also allow us to extend up to events of a larger granularity, such as stages in a relationship. That is, we believe that the results described in earlier sections of this paper can be taken into account in a computational system by maintaining a model of the state of shared and private information across several interactions (several years, if possible). In this way, the shared history of two interlocutors (the user and the system) can be translated into patterns of linguistic behavior, such as reduced use of acknowledgements, and reduced positivity, with increased interruption and information requests. This is similar to Cheng, Cavedon & Dale (2004)'s approach to direction-giving. In this approach, the system maintains a history of places it has given directions to before. Using this *task history*, it is able to generate shorter directions at later stages in the dialogue. In our implementation, however, the very style of the interaction is modified by the shared history of the user and the system. In the sense that we are modifying the linguistic style of the dialogue based on psychological attributes, our approach is similar to work by Mairesse & Walker (2007) and Isard et al. (2006). In both cases, a broad set of natural language generation parameters is employed to generate language that differs along a personality dimension, based on a number of previous empirical studies. In the current approach, however, the features that are modified derive from the interde-

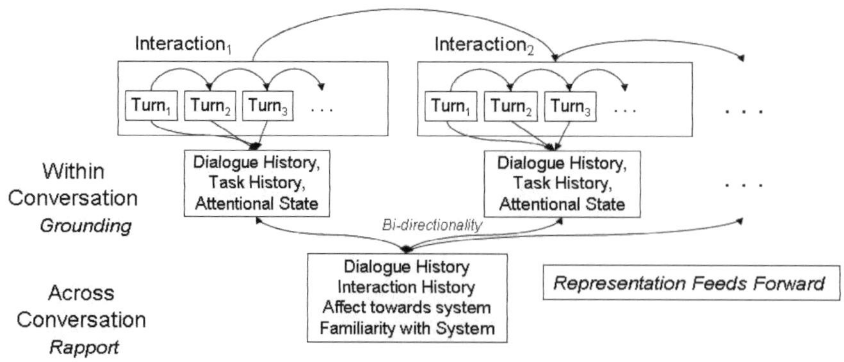

Figure 6. Proposed architecture for modeling coordination within and across conversation

pendence of the system with a particular user.

Some of the features that are present in the conversations of friends, such as interjections and completion of one another's utterances, are still beyond current computational abilities, as they would require online, real-time processing and understanding of utterances with incremental planning and generation of responses. We are interested in pursuing this feature of the system as dialogue technologies improve.

5 Conclusion

In this paper, we have compared direction-giving between friends and strangers, and within these two groups we have compared three subsequent direction-giving episodes. In order to determine the effect played specifically by nonverbal behavior in short- and long-term rapport, half of our participants could see one another, while the other half were divided by a screen. Our experimental and analytic methodology drew from both the social psychological, conversational analysis, and conversation as joint action traditions. Consequently, our results were able to demonstrate the ways in which the verbal and nonverbal devices that index rapport relate to the role those same devices play in knowledge coordination. Based on this commonality, we proposed a computationally viable model of deepening friendship within and across subsequent tasks that extends our previous work on grounding in face-to-face interaction. The work we have presented here therefore differs substantially from previous work on rapport and relationship building in embodied conversational agents. We did not start out with a definition of rapport but instead investigated those behaviors that characterize dyads who have self-identified as friends or strangers. And rather than looking at rapid assessment of rapport (the feeling of "clicking") we looked at the long-term version: acquiring a sense of mutual interdependence. Finally, rather than looking at how to get ECAs to engage users into establishing a relationship, or into letting down their guard, we examined those behaviors that characterize the dyadic interaction at each stage.

All of these topics, however, are clearly interrelated, and future research will benefit from taking a greater number of them into account in both data analysis, and the implementation of ECAs. Future research in our own lab will also have to be more explicit about how to implement the computational model that we have started to lay out here. Additional subjects in a similar experiment will no doubt facilitate that task.

As we increasingly understand better how conversation changes when people come to know one another, we expect to apply these results to our ongoing research on virtual peers that can teach children with autism how to sustain interpersonal relationships (Tartaro & Cassell, 2006) and to our work on building the survey interviewers of the future, who can both engage their survey-takers and keep them honest (Cassell & Miller, in press). More generally, however, we hope to increasingly implement ECAs who will stick around for the long haul.

Acknowledgments

Thanks to Kristina Striegnitz , Will Thompson, Tara Latta and Nate Cantelmo for their help, and Darren Gergle for his superior statistical knowledge. We are grateful to Motorola for funding that supported some of the research reported here.

References

Bickmore, T., & Picard, R. (2005). Establishing and Maintaining Long-Term Human-Computer Relationships. *ACM Transactions on Computer Human Interaction (ToCHI)*, *12*(2), 293-327.

Brown, P., & Levinson, S. (1987). *Politeness: Some Universals in Language Usage*. Studies in International Sociolinguistics. New York: Cambridge University Press.

Cappella, J. N. (1990). On Defining Conversational Coordination and Rapport. *Psychological Inquiry*, *1*(4), 303-305.

Cassell, J., & Bickmore, T. (2002). Negotiated Collusion: Modeling Social Language and its Relationship Effects in Intelligent Agents. *User Modeling and Adaptive Interfaces*, *12*, 1-44.

Cassell, J., & Miller, P. (in press). Is it Self-Administration if the Computer Gives you Encouraging Looks? In F. G. Conrad & M. F. Schober (Eds.), *Envisioning the Survey Interview of the Future*. New York: John Wiley & Sons.

Cassell, J., & Tversky, D. (2005). The Language of Online Intercultural Community Formation. *Journal of Computer-Mediated Communication*, *10*(2), article 2.

Cheng, H., Cavedon, L., & Dale, R. (2004, 28th-29th August). Generating Navigation Information Based on the Driver's Route Knowledge. *Paper presented at the COLING 2004 Workshop on Robust and Adaptive Information Processing for Mobile Speech Interfaces*. Geneva,Switzerland.

Clark, H. H. (1996). *Using Language*. Cambridge: Cambridge University Press.

Clark, H. H., & Brennan, S. E. (1991). Grounding in communication. In L. B. Resnick, J. M. Levine & S. D. Teasley (Eds.), *Perspectives on socially shared cognition* (pp. 127-149). Washington DC: American Psychological Association.

Clark, H. H., & Wilkes-Gibbs, D. (1986). Referring as a collaborative process. *Cognition*, *22*, 1-39.

Core, M., & Allen, J. (1997). Coding Dialogue with the DAMSL Annotation Scheme. *Proceedings of the AAAI Fall Symposium on Communicative Action in Humans and Machines*. Boston, MA.

Duncan, S., Jr. (1990). Measuring Rapport. *Psychological Inquiry*, *1*(4), 310-312.

Goodwin, C. (1981). *Conversational Organization: Interaction between speakers and hearers*. New York: Academic Press.

Grahe, J. E., & Bernieri, F. J. (1999, Win). The importance of nonverbal cues in judging rapport. *Journal of Nonverbal Behavior*, *23*(4), 253-269. http://www.springeronline.com

Gratch, J., Okhmatovskaia, A., Lamothe, F., Marsella, S., Morales, M., van der Werf, R. J., et al. (2006). Virtual Rapport. *Proceedings of the 5th International Conference on Interactive Virtual Agents (IVA)*. Marina del Rey, CA.

Hornstein, G. A. (1982). *Variations in conversational style as a function of the degree of intimacy between members of a dyad*. Unpublished Doctoral, Clark University.

Isard, A., Brockmann, C., & Oberlander, J. (2006). Individuality and alignment in generated dialogues. *Proceedings of the 4th International Natural Language Generation Conference* (pp. 22-29). Sydney, Australia.

Maatman, M., Gratch, J., & Marsella, S. (2005). Natural Behavior of a Listening Agent. *Paper presented at the 5th International Conference on Interactive Virtual Agents (IVA)*. Kos, Greece.

Mairesse, F., & Walker, M. (2007). PERSONAGE: Personality generation for dialogue. *Proceedings of the 45th Annual Meeting of the Association for Computational Linguistics (ACL)*. Prague.

Matheson, C., Poesio, M., & Traum, D. (2000). Modelling Grounding and Discourse Obligations Using Update Rules. *Proceedings of the 1st Annual Meeting of the North American Association for Computational Linguistics (NAACL2000)*. Seattle, WA.

Nakano, Y. I., Reinstein, G., Stocky, T., & Cassell, J. (2003, July 7-12). Towards a Model of Face-to-Face Grounding. *Proceedings of the Annual Meeting of the Association for Computational Linguistics* (p. 553–561). Sapporo, Japan: Association for Computational Linguistics

Rayson, P. (2003). *Matrix: A statistical method and software tool for linguistic analysis through corpus comparison*. Unpublished doctoral thesis, Lancaster University, Lancaster.

Richmond, V. P., & McCroskey, J. C. (1995). Immediacy. In *Nonverbal Behavior in Interpersonal Relations* (pp. 195-217). Boston: Allyn & Bacon.

Schegloff, E. A., & Sacks, H. (1973). Opening up closings. *Semiotica*, *8*, 289-327.

Stronks, B., Nijholt, A., van der Vet, P., & Heylen, D. (2002). Designing for friendship: Becoming friends with your ECA. *Proceedings of the Embodied conversational agents - let's specify and evaluate them!* (pp. 91-97). Bologna, Italy: ACM Press.

Tartaro, A., & Cassell, J. (2006, August 28 - September 1). Authorable virtual peers for autism spectrum disorders. *Proceedings of the Combined workshop on Language-Enabled Educational Technology and Development and Evaluation for Robust Spoken Dialogue Systems at the 17th European Conference on Artificial Intellegence*. Riva Del Garda, Italy.

Tickle-Degnen, L., & Rosenthal, R. (1990). The nature of rapport and its nonverbal correlates. *Psychological Inquiry*, *1*(4), 285-293.

Traum, D. R. (1994). *A Computational Theory of Grounding in Natural Language Conversation*. University of Rochester, Rochester, NY.

Traum, D. R., & Dillenbourg, P. (1998). Towards a Normative Model of Grounding in Collaboration. *Proceedings of the ESSLLI-98 workshop on Mutual Knowledge, Common Ground and Public Information*. Saarbrucken, Germany.

Welji, H., & Duncan, S. (2005). Collaboration and Narration: The role of shared knowledge in the speech and gesture production of friends and strangers. *Paper presented at the International Society of Gesture Studies Conference*. Lyon, France.

Design and Evaluation of an American Sign Language Generator

Matt Huenerfauth
Computer Science Department
CUNY Queens College
The City University of New York
65-30 Kissena Boulevard
Flushing, NY 11375 USA
matt@cs.qc.cuny.edu

Liming Zhao, Erdan Gu, Jan Allbeck
Center for Human Modeling & Simulation
University of Pennsylvania
3401 Walnut Street
Philadelphia, PA 19104 USA
{liming,erdan,allbeck}
@seas.upenn.edu

Abstract

We describe the implementation and evaluation of a prototype American Sign Language (ASL) generation component that produces animations of ASL classifier predicates, some frequent and complex spatial phenomena in ASL that no previous generation system has produced. We discuss some challenges in evaluating ASL systems and present the results of a user-based evaluation study of our system.

1 Background and Motivations

American Sign Language (ASL) is a natural language with a linguistic structure distinct from English used as a primary means of communication for approximately one half million people in the U.S. (Mitchell et al., 2006). A majority of deaf 18-year-olds in the U.S. have an English reading level below that of an average 10-year-old hearing student (Holt, 1991), and so software to translate English text into ASL animations can improve many people's access to information, communication, and services. Previous English-to-ASL machine translation projects (Sáfár & Marshall, 2001; Zhou et al., 2000) could not generate classifier predicates (CPs), phenomena in which signers use special hand movements to indicate the location and movement of invisible objects in space around them (representing entities under discussion). Because CPs are frequent in ASL and necessary for conveying many concepts, we have developed a CP generator that can be incorporated into a full English-to-ASL machine translation system.

During a CP, signers use their hands to position, move, trace, or re-orient imaginary objects in the space in front of them to indicate the location, movement, shape, contour, physical dimension, or some other property of corresponding real world entities under discussion. CPs consist of a semantically meaningful handshape and a 3D hand movement path. A handshape is chosen from a closed set based on characteristics of the entity described (whether it be a vehicle, human, animal, etc.) and what aspect of the entity the signer is describing (surface, position, motion, etc). For example, the sentence "the car parked between the cat and the house" could be expressed in ASL using 3 CPs. First, a signer performs the ASL sign HOUSE while raising her eyebrows (to introduce a new entity as a topic). Then, she moves her hand in a "Spread C" handshape (Figure 1) forward to a point in space where a miniature house could be envisioned. Next, the signer performs the sign CAT with eyebrows raised and makes a similar motion with a "Hooked V" handshape to a location where a cat could be imagined. Finally, she performs the sign CAR (with eyebrows raised) and uses a "Number 3" handshape to trace a path that stops at between the 'house' and the 'cat.' Her other hand makes a flat surface for the 'car' to park on. (Figure 3 will show our system's animation.)

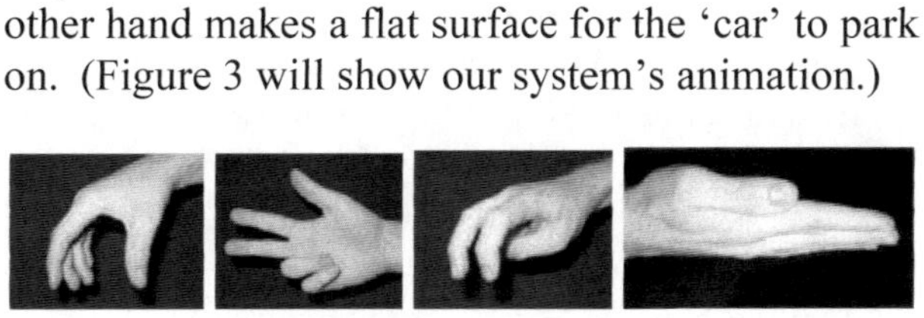

Figure 1: ASL handshapes: Spread C (bulky object), Number 3 (vehicle), Hooked V (animal), Flat (surface).

Proceedings of the Workshop on Embodied Language Processing, pages 51–58,
Prague, Czech Republic, June 28, 2007.

2 System Design and Implementation

We have built a prototype ASL generation module that could be incorporated into an English-to-ASL machine translation system. When given a 3D model of the arrangement of a set of objects whose location and movement should be described in ASL, our system produces an animation of ASL sentences containing classifier predicates to describe the scene. Classifier predicates are the way such spatial information is typically conveyed in ASL. Since this is the first ASL generation system to produce classifier predicate sentences (Huenerfauth, 2006b), we have also conducted an evaluation study in which native ASL signers compared our system's animations to the current state of the art: Signed English animations (described later).

2.1 Modeling the Use of Space

To produce classifier predicates and other ASL expressions that associate locations in space around a signer with entities under discussion, an English-to-ASL system must model what objects are being discussed in an English text, and it must map placeholders for these objects to locations in space around the signer's body. The input to our ASL classifier predicate generator is an explicit 3D model of how a set of placeholders representing discourse entities are positioned in the space around the signing character's body (Huenerfauth, 2006b). This 3D model is "mapped" onto a volume of space in front of the signer's torso, and this model is used to guide the motion of the ASL signer's hands during the performance of classifier predicates describing the motion of these objects

The model encodes the 3D location (center-of-mass) and orientation values of the set of objects that we want to our system describe using ASL animation. For instance, to generate the "car parking between the cat and the house" example, we would pass our system a model with three sets of location (x, y, z coordinates) and orientation (x, y, z, rotation angles) values: for the cat, the car, and the house. Each 3D placeholder also includes a set of bits that represent the set of possible ASL classifier handshapes that can be used to describe it.

While this 3D model is given as input to our prototype classifier predicate generator, when part of a full generation system, virtual reality "scene visualization" software can be used to produce a 3D model of the arrangement and movement of objects discussed in an English input text (Badler et al., 2000; Coyne and Sproat, 2001).

2.2 Template-Based Planning Generation

Given the 3D model above, the system uses a planning-based approach to determine how to move the signer's hands, head-tilt, and eye-gaze to produce an animation of a classifier predicate. The system stores a library of templates representing the various kinds of classifier predicates it may produce. These templates are planning operators (they have logical pre-conditions, monitored termination conditions, and effects), allowing the system to trigger other elements of ASL signing performance that may be required during a grammatically correct classifier predicate (Huenerfauth, 2006b). Each planning operator is parameterized on an object in the 3D model (and its 3D coordinates); for instance, there is a templated planning operator for generating an ASL classifier predicate to show a "parking" event. The specific location/orientation of the vehicle that is parking would be the parameter passed to the planning operator.

There is debate in the ASL linguistics community about the underlying structure of classifier predicates and the generation process by which signers produce them. Our parameterized template approach mirrors one recent linguistic model (Liddell, 2003), and the implementation and evaluation of our prototype generator will help determine whether this was a good choice for our system.

2.3 Multi-Channel Syntax Representation

While strings and syntax trees are used to represent written languages inside of NLP software, these encodings are difficult to adapt to a sign language. ASL lacks a standard writing system, and the multichannel nature of an ASL performance makes it difficult to encode in a linear single-channel string. This project developed a new formalism for representing a linguistic signal in a multi-channel manner and for encoding temporal coordination and non-coordination relationships between portions of the signal (Huenerfauth, 2006a). The output of our planner is a tree-like structure that represents the animation to be synthesized. The tree has two kinds of non-terminal nodes: some indicate that their children should be performed in sequence (like a traditional linguistic syntax tree), and some non-terminals indicate that their children should be performed in parallel (e.g. one child subtree may specify the movement of the arms, and another, the facial expression). In this way, the structure can encode how multiple parts of the sign language performance should be coordinated over time while still leaving flexibility to the exact timing of events – see Figure 2. In earlier work, we have argued that this representation is sufficient for encoding ASL animation (Huenerfauth, 2006a), and the implementation and evaluation of our system (using this formalism) will help test this claim.

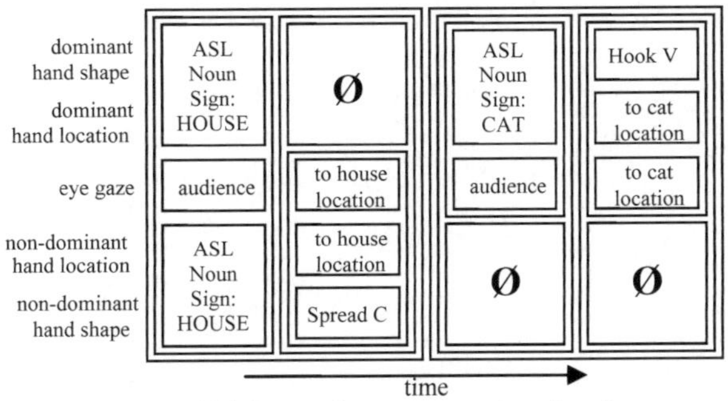

Figure 2: A multichannel representation for the sentence "The cat is next to the house." This example shows handshape, hand location, and eye gaze direction – some details omitted from the example: hand orientation, head tilt, and brow-raising. Changes in timing of individual animation events causes the structure to stretch in the time dimension (like an HTML table).

2.4 Creating Virtual Human Animation

After planning, the system has a tree-structure that specifies activities for parts of the signer's body. Non-terminal nodes indicate whether their children are performed in sequence or in parallel, and the terminal nodes (the inner rectangles in Figure 2) specify animation events for a part of the signer's body. Nodes' time durations are not yet specified (since the human animation component would know the time that movements require, not the linguistic planner). So, the generator queries the human animation system to calculate an estimated time duration for each body animation event (each terminal node), and the structure is then 'balanced' so that if several events are meant to occur in parallel, then the shorter events are 'stretched out.' (The linguistic system can set max/min times for some events prior to the animation processing.)

2.5 Eye-Gaze and Brow Control

The facial model is implemented using the Greta facial animation engine (Pasquariello and Pelachaud, 2001). Our model controls the motion of the signer's eye-brows, which can be placed in a "raised" or "flat" position. The eye motor control repertoire contains three behaviors: fixation on a 3D location in space around the signer's body, smooth pursuit of a moving 3D location, and eye-blinking. Gaze direction is computed from the location values specified inside the 3D model, and the velocity and time duration of the movement are determined by the timing values inside the tree-structure output from the planner. The signer's head tilt changes to accommodate horizontal or vertical gaze shifts greater than a set threshold. When performing a "fixation" or "smooth pursuit" with the eye-gaze, the rate of eye blinking is decreased. Whenever the signer's eye-gaze is not otherwise specified for the animation performance, the default behavior is to look at the audience.

2.6 Planning Arm Movement

Given the tree-structure with animation events, the output of arm-planning should be a list of animation frames that completely specify the rotation angles of the joints of the signer's hands and arms. The hand is specified using 20 rotation angles for the finger joints, and the arm is specified using 9 rotation angles: 2 for the clavicle joint, 3 for the shoulder joint, 1 for the elbow joint, and 3 for the wrist. The linguistic planner specifies the handshape that should be used for specific classifier predicates; however, the tree-structure specifies the arm movements by giving a target location for the center of the signer's palm and a target orientation value for the palm. The system must find a set of clavicle, shoulder, elbow, and wrist angles that get the hand to this desired location and palm orientation. In addition to reaching this target, the arm pose for each animation frame must be as natural as possible, and the animation between frames must be smooth. The system uses an inverse kinematics (IK) which automatically favors natural arm poses. Using the wrist as the end-effector, an elbow angle is selected based on the distance from shoulder to the target, and this elbow angle is fixed. We next compute a set of possible shoulder and wrist rotation angles in order to align the signer's hand with the target palm orientation. Disregarding elbow angles that force impossible wrist joint angles, we select the arm pose that is collision free and is the most natural, according to a shoulder strength model (Zhao et al., 2005).

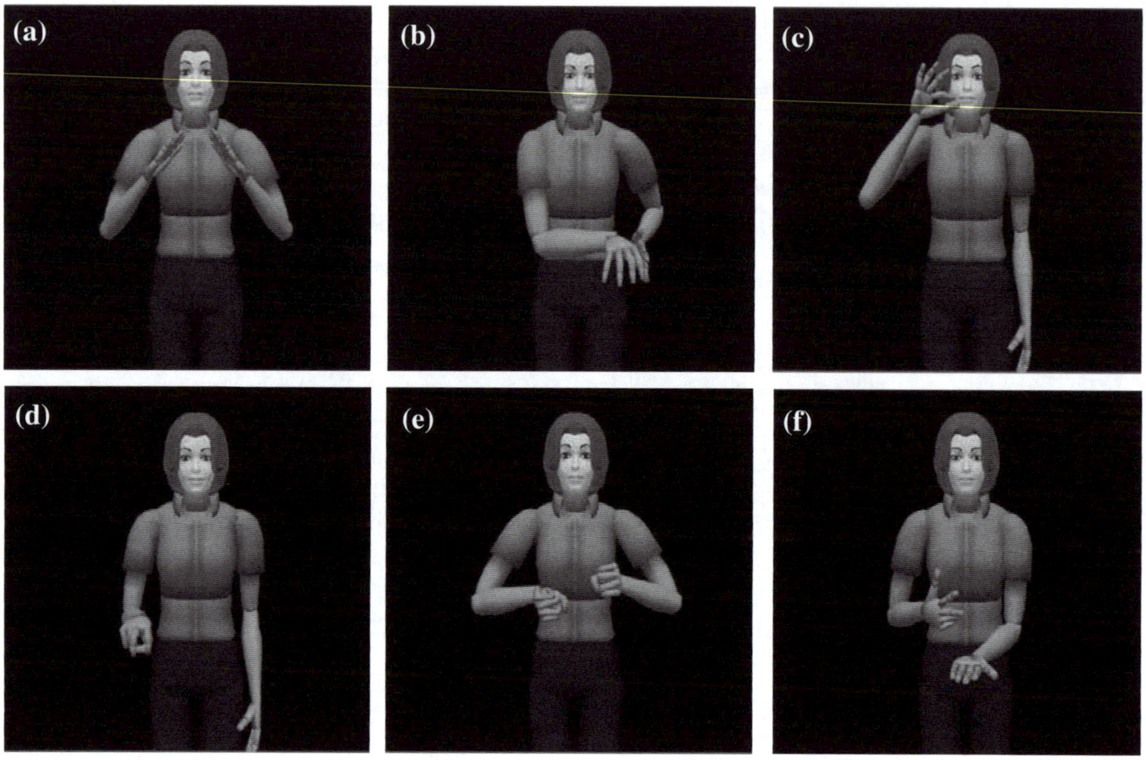

Figure 3: Images from our system's animation of a classifier predicate for "the car parked between the house and the cat." (a) ASL sign HOUSE, eyes at audience, brows raised; (b) Spread C handshape and eye gaze to house location; (c) ASL sign CAT, eyes at audience, brows raised; (d) Hooked V handshape and eye gaze to cat location; (e) ASL sign CAR, eyes at audience, brows raised; (f) Number 3 handshape (for the car) parks atop Flat handshape while the eye gaze tracks the movement path of the car.

2.7 Synthesizing Virtual Human Animation

This animation specification is performed by an animated human character in the Virtual Human Testbed (Badler et al., 2005). Because the Greta system used a female head with light skin tone, a female human body was chosen with matching skin. The character was dressed in a blue shirt and pants that contrasted with its skin tone. To make the character appear to be a conversational partner, the "camera" inside the virtual environment was set at eye-level with the character and at an appropriate distance for ASL conversation.

2.8 Coverage of the Prototype System

Our prototype system can be used to translate a limited range of English sentences (discussing the locations and movements of a small set of people or objects) into animations of an onscreen human-like character performing ASL classifier predicates to convey the locations and movements of the entities in the English text. Table 1 includes shorthand transcripts of some ASL sentence animations produced by the system; the first sentence corresponds to the classifier predicate animation in Figure 3.

3 Issues in Evaluating ASL Generation

There has been little work on developing evaluation methodologies for sign language generation or MT systems. Some have shown how automatic string-based evaluation metrics fail to identify correct sign language translations (Morrisey and Way, 2006), and they propose building large parallel written/sign corpora containing more syntactic and semantic information (to enable more sophisticated metrics to be created). Aside from the expense of creating such corpora, we feel that there are several factors that motivate user-based evaluation studies for sign language generation systems – especially for those systems that produce classifier predicates. These factors include some unique linguistic properties of sign languages and the lack of standard writing systems for most sign languages, like ASL.

Most automatic evaluation approaches for generation or MT systems compare a string produced by a system to a human-produced "gold-standard" string. Sign languages usually lack written forms that are commonly used or known among signers. While we could invent an artificial ASL writing system for the generator to produce as output (for evaluation purposes only), it's not clear that human ASL signers could accurately or consistently produce written forms of ASL sentences to serve as "gold standards" for such an evaluation. Further, real users of the system would never be shown artificial written ASL; they would see animation output. Thus, evaluations based on strings would not test the full process – including the synthesis of the "string" into an animation – when errors may arise.

Another reason why string-based evaluation metrics are not well-suited to ASL is that sign languages have linguistic properties that can confound string-edit-distance-based metrics. ASL consists of the coordinated movement of several parts of the body in parallel (i.e. face, eyes, head, hands), and so a string listing the set of signs performed is a lossy representation of the original performance (Huenerfauth, 2006a). The string may not encode the non-manual parts of the sentence, and so string-based metrics would fail to consider those important aspects. Discourse factors (e.g. topicalization) can also result in movement phenomena in ASL that may scramble the sequence of signs in the sentence without substantially changing its semantics; such movement would affect string-based metrics significantly though the sentence meaning may change little. The use of head-tilt and eye-gaze during the performance of ASL verb signs may also license the dropping of entire sentence constituents (Neidle et. al, 2000). The entities discussed are associated with locations in space around the signer at which head-tilt or eye-gaze is aimed, and thus the constituent is actually still expressed although no manual signs are performed for it. Thus, an automatic metric may penalize such a sentence (for missing a constituent) while the information is still there. Finally, ASL classifier predicates convey a lot of information in a single complex 'sign' (handshape indicates semantic category, movement shows 3D path/rotation), and it is unclear how we could "write" the 3D data of a classifier predicate in a string-based encoding or how to calculate an edit-distance between a 'gold standard' classifier predicate and a generated one.

4 Evaluation of the System

We used a user-based evaluation methodology in which human native ASL signers are shown the output of our generator and asked to rate each animation on ten-point scales for understandability, naturalness of movement, and ASL grammatical correctness. To evaluate whether the animation conveyed the proper semantics, signers were also asked to complete a matching task. After viewing a classifier predicate animation produced by the system, signers were shown three short animations showing the movement or location of the set of objects that were described by the classifier predicate. The movement of the objects in each animation was slightly different, and signers were asked to select which of the three animations depicted the scene that was described by the classifier predicate.

Since this prototype is the first generator to produce animations of ASL classifier predicates, there are no other systems to compare it to in our study. To create a lower baseline for comparison, we wanted a set of animations that reflect the current state of the art in broad-coverage English-to-sign

English Gloss	ASL Sentence with Classifier Predicates (CPs)	Signed English Sentence
The car parks between the house and the cat.	ASL sign HOUSE; CP: house location; sign CAT; CP: cat location; sign CAR; CP: car path.	THE CAR PARK BETWEEN THE HOUSE AND THE CAT
The man walks next to the woman.	ASL sign WOMAN; CP: woman location; sign MAN; CP: man path.	THE MAN WALK NEXT-TO THE WOMAN
The car turns left.	ASL sign CAR; CP: car path.	THE CAR TURN LEFT
The lamp is on the table.	ASL sign TABLE; CP: table location; sign LIGHT; CP: lamp location.	THE LIGHT IS ON THE TABLE
The tree is near the tent.	ASL sign TENT; CP: tent location; sign TREE; CP: tree location.	THE TREE IS NEAR THE TENT
The man walks between the tent and the frog.	ASL sign TENT; CP: tent location; sign FROG; CP: frog location; sign MAN; CP: man path.	THE MAN WALK BETWEEN THE TENT AND THE FROG
The man walks away from the woman.	ASL sign WOMAN: CP: woman location; sign MAN; CP: man path.	THE MAN WALK FROM THE WOMAN
The car drives up to the house.	ASL sign HOUSE; CP: house location; sign CAR; CP: car path.	THE CAR DRIVE TO THE HOUSE
The man walks up to the woman.	ASL sign WOMAN; CP: woman location; sign MAN; CP: man path.	THE MAN WALK TO THE WOMAN
The woman stands next to the table.	ASL sign TABLE; CP: table location; sign WOMAN; CP: woman location.	THE WOMAN STAND NEXT-TO THE TABLE

Table 1: ASL and Signed English sentences included in the evaluation study (with English glosses).

translation. Since there are no broad-coverage English-to-*ASL* MT systems, we used Signed English transliterations as our lower baseline. Signed English is a form of communication in which each word of an English sentence is replaced with a corresponding sign, and the sentence is presented in original English word order without any accompanying ASL linguistic features such as meaningful facial expressions or eye-gaze.

Ten ASL animations (generated by our system) were selected for inclusion in this study based on some desired criteria. The ASL animations consist of classifier predicates of movement and location – the focus of our research. The categories of people and objects discussed in the sentences require a variety of ASL handshapes to be used. Some sentences describe the location of objects, and others describe movement. The sentences describe from one to three objects in a scene, and some pairs of sentences actually discuss the same set of objects, but moving in different ways. Since the creation of a referring expression generator was not a focus of our prototype, all referring expressions in the animations are simply an ASL noun phrase consisting of a single sign – some one-handed and some two-handed. Table 1 lists the ten classifier predicate animations we selected (with English glosses).

For the "matching task" portion of the study, three animated visualizations were created for each sentence showing how the objects mentioned in the sentence move in 3D. One animation was an accurate visualization of the location/movement of the objects, and the other two animations were "confusables" – showing orientations/movements for the objects that did not match the classifier predicate animations. Because we wanted to evaluate

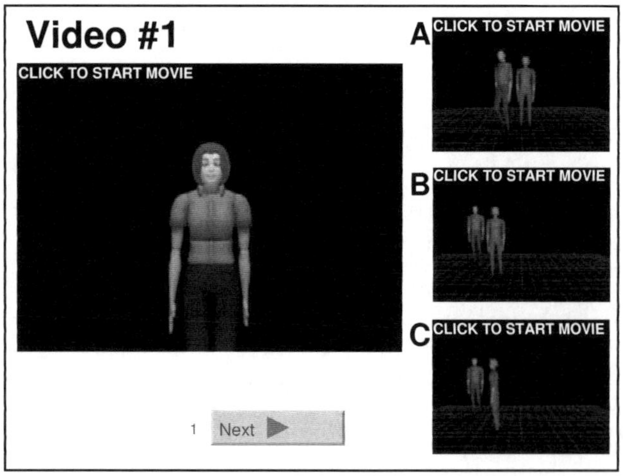

Figure 4: Screenshot from evaluation program.

the classifier predicates (and not the referring expressions), the set of objects that appeared in all three visualizations for a sentence was the same. Thus, it was the movement and orientation information conveyed by the classifier predicate (and not the object identity conveyed by the referring expression) that would distinguish the correct visualization from the confusables. For example, the following three visualizations were created for the sentence "the car parks between the cat and the house" (the cat and house remain in the same location in each): (1) a car drives on a curved path and parks at a location between a house and a cat, (2) a car drives between a house and a cat but continues driving past them off camera, and (3) a car starts at a location between a house and a cat and drives to a location that is not between them anymore.

To create the Signed English animations for each sentence, some additional signs were added to the generator's library of signs. (ASL does not traditionally use signs such as "THE" that are used in Signed English.) A sequence of signs for each Signed English transliteration was concatenated, and the synthesis sub-component of our system was used to calculate smooth transitional movements for the arms and hands between each sign in the sentence. The glosses for the ten Signed English transliterations are also listed in Table 1.

4.1 User-Interface for Evaluation Study

An interactive slideshow was created with one slide for each of the 20 animations (10 from our ASL system, 10 Signed English). On each slide, the signing animation was shown on the left of the screen, and the three possible visualizations of that sentence were shown to the right (see Figure 4). The slides were placed in a random order for each of the participants in the study. A user could replay the animations as many times as desired before going to the next signing animation. Subjects were asked to rate each of these animations on a 1-to-10-point scale for ASL grammatical correctness, understandability, and naturalness of movement. Subjects were also asked to select which of the three animated visualizations (choice "A," "B," or "C") matched the scene as described in the sentence performed by the virtual character.

After these slides, 3 more slides appeared containing animations from our generator. (These were repeats of 3 animations used in the main part of the study.) These three slides only showed the "correct" animated visualization for that sentence. For these last three slides, subjects were instead asked to comment on the animation's speed, colors/lighting, hand visibility, correctness of hand movement, facial expression, and eye-gaze. Signers were also asked to write any comments they had about how the animation should be improved.

4.2 Recruitment and Screening of Subjects

Subjects were recruited through personal contacts in the deaf community who helped identify friends, family, and associates who met the screening criteria. Participants had to be native ASL signers – many deaf individuals are non-native signers who learned ASL later in life (and may accept English-like signing as being grammatical ASL). Subjects were preferred who had learned ASL since birth, had deaf parents that used ASL at home, and/or attending a residential school for the deaf as a child (where they were immersed in an ASL-signing community). Of our 15 subjects, 8 met all three criteria, 2 met two criteria, and 5 met one (1 grew up with ASL-signing deaf parents and 4 attended a residential school for the deaf from an early age).

During the study, instructions were given to participants in ASL, and a native signer was present during 13 of the 15 sessions to answer questions or to explain experimental procedures. This signer engaged the participants in conversation in ASL before the session to produce an ASL-immersive environment. Participants were given instructions in ASL about how to score each category. For grammaticality, they were told that "perfect ASL grammar" would be a 10, but "mixed-up" or "English-like" grammar should be a 1. For understandability, "easy to understand" sentences should be a 10, but "confusing" sentences should be a 1. For naturalness, animations in which the signer moved "smoothly, like a real person" should be a 10, but animations in which the signer moved in a "choppy" manner "like a robot" should be a 1.

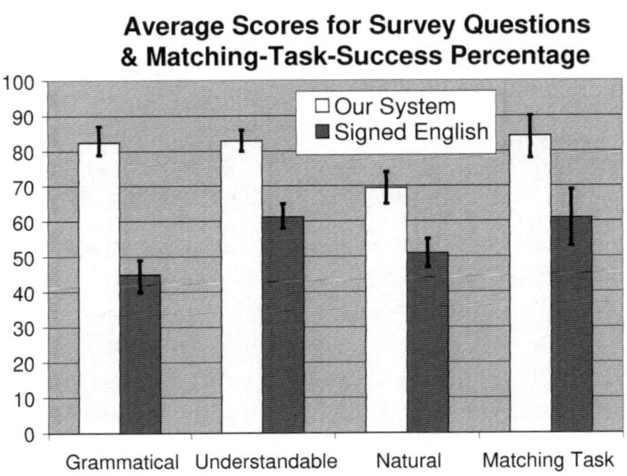

Figure 5: Grammaticality, understandability, naturalness, and matching-task-success scores.

4.3 Results of the Evaluation

Figure 5 shows average scores for grammaticality, understandability, naturalness, and matching-task-success percentage for the animations from our system compared to the Signed English animations. Our system's higher scores in all categories is significant ($\alpha = 0.05$, pairwise Mann-Whitney U tests with Bonferonni-corrected p-values).

Subjects were asked to comment on the animation speed, color, lighting, visibility of the hands, correctness of hand movement, correctness of facial expressions, correctness of eye-gaze, and other ways of improving the animations. Of the 15 subjects, eight said that some animations were a little slow, and one felt some were very slow. Eight subjects wanted the animations to have more facial expressions, and 4 of these specifically mentioned nose and mouth movements. Four subjects said the signer's body should seem more loose/relaxed or that it should move more. Two subjects wanted the signer to show more emotion. Two subjects felt that eye-brows should go higher when raised, and three felt there should be more eye-gaze movements. Two subjects felt the blue color of the signer's shirt was a little too bright, and one disliked the black background. Some subjects commented on particular ASL signs that they felt were performed incorrectly. For example, three discussed the sign "FROG": one felt it should be performed a little more to the right of its current location, and another felt that the hand should be oriented with the fingers aimed more to the front. Some participants commented on the classifier predicate portions of the performance. For example, in the sentence "the car parked between the cat and the house," one subject felt it would be better to use the non-dominant hand to hold the location of the house during the car's movement instead of using the non-dominant hand to create a platform for the dominant hand (the car) to park upon.

5 Conclusions and Future Work

Unlike an evaluation of a broad-coverage NLP system, during which we obtain performance statistics for the system as it carries out a linguistic task on a large corpus or "test set," this paper has described an evaluation of a prototype system. We were not measuring the linguistic coverage of the system but rather its functionality. Did signers agree that the animation output: (1) is actually a grammatically-correct and understandable classifier predicate and (2) conveys the information about the movement of objects in the 3D scene being described? We expected to find animation details that could be improved in future work; however, since there are currently no other systems capable of generating ASL classifier predicate animations, any system receiving an answer of "yes" to questions (1) and (2) above is an improvement to the state of the art.

Another contribution of this initial evaluation is that it serves as a pilot study to help us determine how to better evaluate sign language generation systems in the future. We found that subjects were comfortable critiquing ASL animations, and most suggested specific (and often subtle) elements of the animation to be improved. Their feedback suggested new modifications we can make to the system (and then evaluate again in future studies). Because subjects gave such high quality feedback, future studies will also elicit such comments.

During the study, we also experimented with recording a native ASL signer (using a motion-capture suit and datagloves) performing classifier predicates. We tried to use this motion-capture data to animate a virtual human character superficially identical to the one used by our system. We hoped that this character controlled by human movements could serve as an upper-baseline in the evaluation study. Unfortunately, the motion-capture data we collected contained minor errors that required post-processing clean-up, and the resulting animations contained enough movement inaccuracies that native ASL signers who viewed them felt they were actually less understandable than our system's animations. In future work, we intend to explore alternative upper-baselines to compare our system's animations to: animation from alternative motion-capture techniques, hand-coded animations based on a human's performance, or simply a video of a human signer performing ASL sentences.

Acknowledgements

National Science Foundation Award #0520798 "SGER: Generating Animations of American Sign Language Classifier Predicates" (Universal Access, 2005) supported this work. Software was donated by UGS Tecnomatix and Autodesk. Thank you to Mitch Marcus, Martha Palmer, and Norman Badler.

References

N.I. Badler, J. Allbeck, S.J. Lee, R.J. Rabbitz, T.T. Broderick, and K.M. Mulkern. 2005. New behavioral paradigms for virtual human models. SAE Digital Human Modeling.

N. Badler, R. Bindiganavale, J. Allbeck, W. Schuler, L. Zhao, S. Lee, H. Shin, & M. Palmer. 2000. Parameterized action representation & natural language instructions for dynamic behavior modification of embodied agents. AAAI Spring.

R. Coyne and R. Sproat. 2001. WordsEye: an automatic text-to-scene conversion system. ACM SIGGRAPH.

J.A. Holt. 1991. Demographic, Stanford Achievement Test - 8th Edition for Deaf and Hard of Hearing Students: Reading Comprehension Subgroup Results.

É . Sáfár & I. Marshall. 2001. The architecture of an English-text-to-Sign-Languages translation system. Recent Advances in Natural Language Processing.

Matt Huenerfauth. In Press. Representing American Sign Language classifier predicates using spatially parameterized planning templates. In M. Banich and D. Caccamise (Eds.), *Generalization.* Mahwah: LEA.

Matt Huenerfauth. 2006a. Representing Coordination and Non-Coordination in American Sign Language Animations. *Behaviour & Info. Technology*, 25:4.

Matt Huenerfauth. 2006b. Generating American Sign Language Classifier Predicates for English-to-ASL Machine Translation. Dissertation, U. Pennsylvania.

Liddell, S. 2003. Grammar, Gesture, and Meaning in American Sign Language. UK: Cambridge U. Press.

R.E. Mitchell, T.A. Young, B. Bachleda, & M.A. Karchmer. 2006. How Many People Use ASL in the United States? Why estimates need updating. *Sign Language Studies*, 6:3.

S. Morrissey & A. Way. 2006. Lost in Translation: The problems of using mainstream MT evaluation metrics for sign language translation. *5th SALTMIL Workshop on Minority Languages, LREC-200*

C. Neidle, J. Kegl, D. MacLaughlin, B. Bahan, & R.G. Lee. 2000. *The Syntax of American Sign Language: Functional Categories and Hierarchical Structure.* Cambridge: MIT.

S. Pasquariello & C. Pelachaud. 2001. Greta: A simple facial animation engine. In 6th Online World Conference on Soft Computing in Industrial Applications.

L. Zhao, K. Kipper, W. Schuler, C. Vogler, N.I. Badler, & M. Palmer. 2000. Machine Translation System from English to American Sign Language. Assoc. for MT in the Americas.

L. Zhao, Y. Liu, N.I. Badler. 2005. Applying empirical data on upper torso movement to real-time collision-free reach tasks. SAE Digital Human Modeling.

Dynamic Movement and Positioning of Embodied Agents in Multiparty Conversations

Dušan Jan
USC Institute for Creative Technologies
13274 Fiji Way
Marina del Rey, CA 90292
jan@ict.usc.edu

David R. Traum
USC Institute for Creative Technologies
13274 Fiji Way
Marina del Rey, CA 90292
traum@ict.usc.edu

Abstract

For embodied agents to engage in realistic multiparty conversation, they must stand in appropriate places with respect to other agents and the environment. When these factors change, for example when an agent joins a conversation, the agents must dynamically move to a new location and/or orientation to accommodate. This paper presents an algorithm for simulating the movement of agents based on observed human behavior using techniques developed for pedestrian movement in crowd simulations. We extend a previous group conversation simulation to include an agent motion algorithm. We examine several test cases and show how the simulation generates results that mirror real-life conversation settings.

1 Introduction

When we look at human conversation in a casual, open setting, such as a party or marketplace, one of the first things we notice is a tendency for people to cluster into sub-groups involved in different conversations. These groupings are not fixed, however, people will often join and leave groups and often move from one group to another. Groups themselves may fragment into subgroups, and smaller groups sometimes merge into one larger group. Participants in these groups adapt their positions and orientations to account for these circumstances, often without missing a beat or otherwise disrupting their conversations.

In order to create believable social environments for games or training simulations we need agents that can perform these same kinds of behaviors in a realistic way. There are a number of crowd simulations (Sung et al., 2004; Shao and Terzopoulos, 2005; Still, 2000; Helbing and Molnár, 1995), but most of these place an emphasis on large-scale movement of agents and do not model the low-level aspects of conversational interaction in a realistic way — movement of agents in multiparty conversation is more about positioning and repositioning on a local scale. There is also a large body of work on embodied conversational agents (Cassell et al., 2000), which attempt to model realistic conversational non-verbal behaviors. Most of this work focuses on aspects such as gaze, facial expressions, and hand and arm gestures, rather than positioning and orientation in a group. There is some important work on authored presentation agents and avatars for human participants which take account of position in the modelling (Vilhjalmsson and Cassell, 1998; Rehm et al., 2005), but none of this work presents fully explicit algorithms for controlling the positioning and movement behavior of autonomous agents in dynamic conversations.

In previous work, it has been shown that incorrect positioning of animated agents has a negative effect on the believability of dynamic group conversation (Jan and Traum, 2005). Research from anthropologists and social psychologists such as the classic work on proxemics by Hall (1968) and positioning by Kendon (1990) provide social reasons to explain how people position themselves in different situations. It is also important to know that people expect

Proceedings of the Workshop on Embodied Language Processing, pages 59–66,
Prague, Czech Republic, June 28, 2007. ©2007 Association for Computational Linguistics

similar behavior in virtual environments as in real life as shown by Bailenson et al. (2003). This gives us basic principles on which to base the simulation and provides some qualitative expectations, but is not suitable to directly convert into algorithms. The social force model (Helbing and Molnár, 1995) developed for crowd simulations gives a good framework for movement simulation. While the basic model shows how to handle pedestrian motion we apply the model to the problem of movement in conversation setting.

Our implementation of conversational movement and positioning is an extension of prior work in group conversation simulation using autonomous agents. Carletta and Padilha (2002) presented a simulation of the external view of a group conversation, in which the group members take turns speaking and listening to others. Previous work on turn-taking is used to form a probabilistic algorithm in which agents can perform basic behaviors such as speaking and listening, beginning, continuing or concluding a speaking turn, giving positive and negative feedback, head nods, gestures, posture shifts, and gaze. Behaviors are generated using a stochastic algorithm that compares randomly generated numbers against parameters that can take on values between 0 and 1.

This work was further extended by (Jan and Traum, 2005), who used new bodies in the Unreal Tournament game engine, and added support for dynamic creation of conversation groups. This simulation allowed dynamic creation, splitting, joining, entry and exit of sub-conversations. However, the characters were located in fixed positions. As indicated in their subject evaluations, this significantly decreased believability when conversation groups did not coincide with positioning of the agents. Adding support for movement of characters is a natural step to counter these less believable situations. We augment this work by adding a movement and positioning component that allows agents to monitor "forces" that make it more desirable to move to one place or another, iteratively select new destinations and move while remaining engaged in conversations.

The rest of the paper is organized as follows. Section 2 describes the main motivations that agents have for moving from their current position in conversation. Section 3 presents the social force model, which specifies a set of forces that pressure an agent to move in one direction or another, and a decision algorithm for deciding which forces to act on in different situations. Section 4 presents a series of test cases for the algorithm, demonstrating that the model behaves as desired for some benchmark problems in this space. We conclude in section 5 with a description of future work in this area.

2 Reasons for Movement

There are several reasons why someone engaged in conversation would want to shift position. Some of these include:

- one is listening to a speaker who is too far and or not loud enough to hear,
- there is too much noise from other nearby sound sources,
- the background noise is louder than the speaker,
- one is too close to others to feel comfortable,
- one has an occluded view or is occluding the view of others.

Any of these factors (or a combination of several) could motivate a participant to move to a more comfortable location. During the simulation the speakers can change, other noise sources can start and stop, and other agents can move around as well. These factors can cause a variety of motion throughout the course of interactions with others. In the rest of this section we describe these factors in more detail. In the next section we will develop a formal model of reactions to these factors.

The first reason we consider for repositioning of conversation participants is audibility of the speaker. The deciding factor can be either the absolute volume of the speaker, or the relative volume compared to other "noise". Noise here describes all audio input that is not speech by someone in the current conversation group. This includes the speech of agents engaged in other conversations as well as non-speech sounds. When we are comparing the loudness of different sources we take into account that intensity of the perceived signal decreases with the square of the distance and also that the loudness of several sources is additive.

Even when the speaker can be heard over a noise source, if outside disruptions are loud enough, the group might want to move to a more remote area where they can interact without interruptions. Each of the participants may decide to shift away from a noise source, even without an explicit group decision. Of course this may not always be possible if the area is very crowded.

Another reason for movement is proxemics. Hall (1968) writes that individuals generally divide their personal space into four distinct zones. The intimate zone is used for embracing or whispering, the personal zone is used for conversation among good friends, the social zone is used for conversation among acquaintances and the public zone for public speaking. The actual distances the zones span are different for each culture and its interpretation may vary based on an individual's personality. If the speaker is outside the participant's preferred zone, the participant will move toward the speaker. Similarly if someone invades the personal zone of a participant, the participant will move away.

The final reason for movement is specific to multiparty conversations. When there are several people in conversation they will tend to form a circular formation. This gives the sense of inclusion to participants and gives them a better view of one another (Kendon, 1990).

3 Social Force Model

We present our movement simulation in the context of a social force model. Similar to movement in crowds, the movement of people engaged in conversation is to a large extent reactionary. The reaction is usually automatic and determined by person's experience, rather than planned for. It is possible to assign a vectorial quantity for each person in conversation, that describes the desired movement direction. This quantity can be interpreted as a social force. This force represents the influence of the environment on the behavior of conversation participant. It is important to note however that this force does not directly cause the body to move, but rather provides a motivation to move. We illustrate these forces with figures such as Figure 1, where each circle represents an agent, the different shadings represent members of different conversation groups, thicker circles represent speakers in that group, and arrows represent forces on an agent of interest.

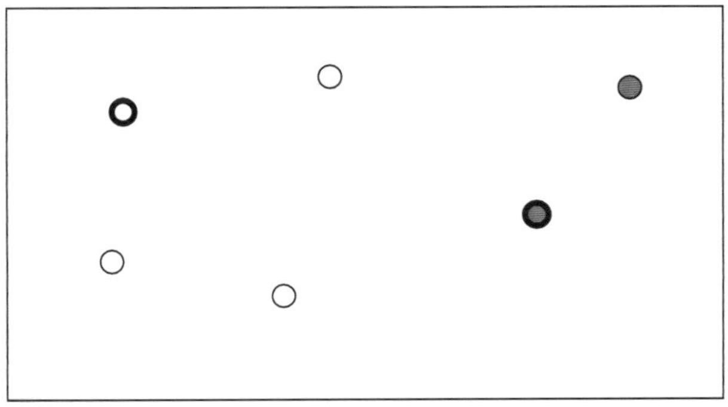

Figure 1: A sample group positioning. Each circle represents an agent. A thick border represents that the agent is talking, filled or empty shading indicates conversation group membership.

We associate a force with each reason for movement:

$\vec{F}_{speaker}$: attractive force toward a speaker

$\vec{F}_{noise}$: repelling force from outside noise

$\vec{F}_{proximity}$: repelling force from agents that are too close

$\vec{F}_{circle}$: force toward circular formation of all conversation participants

$\vec{F}_{speaker}$ is a force that is activated when the speaker is too far from the listener. This can happen for one of two reasons. Either the speaker is not loud enough and the listener has to move closer in order to understand him, or he is outside the desired zone for communication. When the agent decides to join conversation this is the main influence that guides the agent to his conversation group as shown in Figure 2. $\vec{F}_{speaker}$ is computed according to the following equation, where $\vec{r}_{speaker}$ is location of the speaker, $\vec{r}$ is location of the agent and k is a scaling factor (we are currently using $k = 1$):

$$\vec{F}_{speaker} = k(\vec{r}_{speaker} - \vec{r})$$

$\vec{F}_{noise}$ is a sum of forces away from each source of noise. Each component force is directed away from

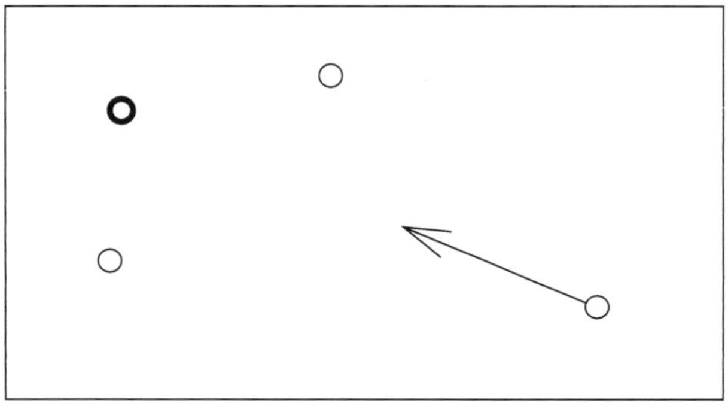

Figure 2: Attractive force toward speaker $\vec{F}_{speaker}$.

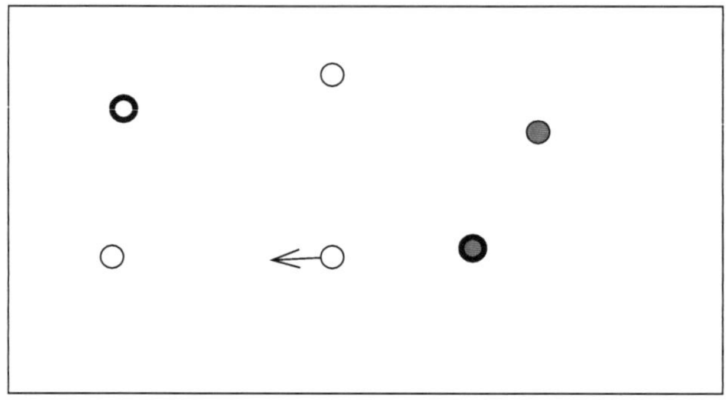

Figure 3: Repelling force away from other speakers $\vec{F}_{noise}$.

that particular source and its size is inversely proportional to square of the distance. This means that only sources relatively close to the agent will have a significant influence. Not all noise is a large enough motivation for the agent to act upon. The force is only active when the noise level exceeds a threshold or when its relative value compared to speaker level in the group exceeds a threshold. Figure 3 shows an example of the latter. The following equation is used to compute $\vec{F}_{noise}$:

$$\vec{F}_{noise} = -\sum_i \frac{\vec{r_i} - \vec{r}}{\|\vec{r_i} - \vec{r}\|^3}$$

$\vec{F}_{proximity}$ is also a cumulative force. It is a sum of forces away from each agent that is too close. The force gets stronger the closer the invading agent is. This takes effect for both agents in the conversation group and other agents. This is the second force that is modeling proxemics. While $\vec{F}_{speaker}$ is activated when the agent is farther than the desired social zone, $\vec{F}_{proximity}$ is activated when the agent moves to a closer zone. Based on how well the agents know each other this can be either when the agent enters the intimate zone or the personal zone. Figure 4 shows an example when two agents get too close to each other. The following equation is used to compute values for $\vec{F}_{proximity}$:

$$\vec{F}_{proximity} = - \sum_{\|\vec{r_i}-\vec{r}\|<distance_{zone}} \frac{\vec{r_i} - \vec{r}}{\|\vec{r_i} - \vec{r}\|^2}$$

$\vec{F}_{circle}$ is responsible for forming the conversational group into a convex, roughly circular formation. Each agent has a belief about who is currently

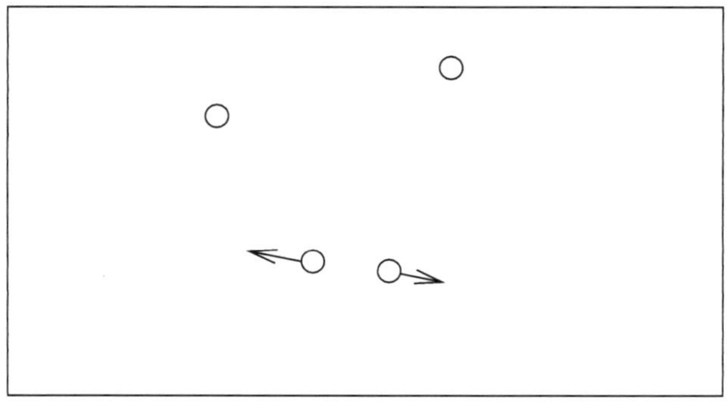

Figure 4: Repelling force away from agents that are too close $\vec{F}_{proximity}$.

participating in the conversation. An agent will compute the center of mass of all these assumed participants and the average distance from the center. If an agent's position deviates too much from the average, the $\vec{F}_{circle}$ gets activated either toward or away from center of mass. Notice that $\vec{F}_{proximity}$ takes care of spreading out around the circle. The situation in Figure 5 is an example where an agent decides that he has to adapt his positioning. Notice that if this agent was not aware of the agent to his left, the force would not get triggered. This can be a cause for many interesting situations when agents have different beliefs about who is part of the conversation.

$$\vec{r}_m = \frac{1}{N}\sum_i \vec{r_i}$$

$$\vec{F}_{circle} = \lambda \left(\frac{1}{N}\sum_i \|\vec{r_i} - \vec{r}_m\| \frac{\vec{r} - \vec{r}_m}{\|\vec{r} - \vec{r}_m\|} - \vec{r} \right)$$

As described above, each force has some conditions that determine whether the force plays an ac-

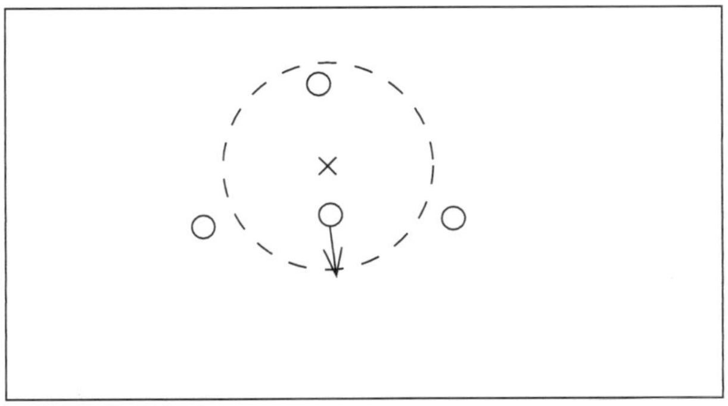

Figure 5: Agent's deviation from circular formation exceeds threshold and triggers force $\vec{F}_{circle}$.

tive role in motivating movement. Since the forces are not actually physically acting on agent's bodies, it is not unreasonable for agents to suppress a certain force. All the possible causes for movement are always present, but the agents selectively decide which ones they will act upon in a given situation. This is unlike a kinematics calculation with physical forces where all forces are always active. Combining all the conditions we can define which forces are active according to a simple decision procedure. We can view this as priorities the agent has that decide which conditions are more important to react to.

In our implementation we use the following priorities:

if speaker is too low $\vec{F} = \vec{F}_{speaker} + \vec{F}_{proximity}$

else if noise is louder than speaker $\vec{F} = \vec{F}_{speaker} + \vec{F}_{noise} + \vec{F}_{proximity}$

else if noise is too loud $\vec{F} = \vec{F}_{noise} + \vec{F}_{proximity}$

else if too close to someone $\vec{F} = \vec{F}_{proximity}$

otherwise $\vec{F} = \vec{F}_{circle}$

Using the above priorities we have a force defined at each point in space where an agent could be located. We do not use this for the continuous computation of movement, but rather use it to compute destination points. In each planning cycle the agents will consider whether they should move. To do this an agent considers his position in the force field and computes a destination in the direction of the force field. This process is performed iteratively a constant *bound* times (unless there is no movement in an earlier iteration). This is described in the following equations, where $\vec{r}$ is the initial position, α is a scaling factor, and $\vec{P}_{bound}$ is the destination for the movement of this planning cycle:

$$\vec{P}_0 = \vec{r}$$
$$\vec{P}_{i+1} = \vec{P}_i + \alpha \vec{F}(\vec{P}_i)$$
$$Destination = \vec{P}_{bound}$$

Once we have computed the destination, we use it as a destination point for the character movement algorithms in the Unreal Tournament game engine. These will manage character animation and collision avoidance.

Figure 6 shows an example with two separate conversation groups, where one agent decides to leave the shaded group and join the unshaded conversation. The figure shows the iterations he is performing in his planning cycle and the resulting final destination.

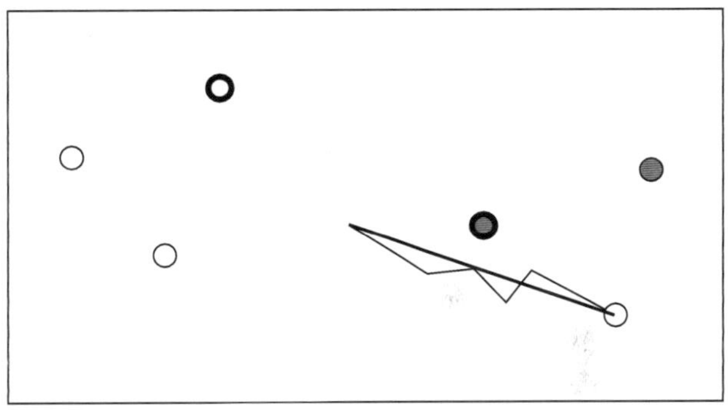

Figure 6: Example of motion computation: The lower right agent decided to join the unshaded conversation. He iteratively applies movement in the direction of local forces. In each iteration the effects of different component forces may take effect. The thick line indicates the final destination and path the agent chooses for this planning cycle.

4 Test Case Analysis

A full evaluation of the social-force based positioning algorithm presented in the previous section would involve analysis of simulations to see if they improve believability over static simulations such as simulation of Jan and Traum (2005), or other algorithms. While this remains future work for the moment, we did evaluate the algorithms against a series of test cases where we know what behavior to expect from known forces. In this section we present three such cases, showing that the algorithm does have the power to represent several aspects of conversational positioning.

In the simulations we describe here we did not change the conversational attributes of agents, but we did constrain the grouping dynamics. In a normal situation the agents would randomly form conversation groups, based on their stochastic decisions. Here we wanted to examine particular scenarios and how the movement algorithm would react to specific changes in conversation group structure. For this reason we disabled conversational grouping decisions in the algorithm and triggered the group structure changes manually from the user interface.

The only variable input to the movement algorithms for different agents is the preferences for proxemics. Each agent has defined values for all zones, but we set all agents to use social zone for communicating. The other parameters such as thresholds for hearing a speaker and noise and circular formations were fixed for these experiments.

4.1 Joining conversation

In this test case we have 4 agents. In the initial condition three agents are engaged in conversation while the fourth one is away from the scene. We let the simulation run and at some point we give a command to the fourth agent to join the group of three. At first the agent will move toward the group until he is in a comfortable range as shown in Figure 7.

At the point in which the fourth agent decides to join the other three, he is the only one who knows he wants to join the conversation. The other agents know of the presence of the fourth agent, but they have no idea that he would like to join them. The fourth agent is listening for a while and when he gives a feedback signal the other agents interpret that as a signal that he wants to join the conversation. As a result the agents reevaluate their positioning and one agent decides it would be appropriate to move a step back to give more space to the new agent. Given more space the new agent is able to move in circular formation with the rest of the group without intruding on the personal zones of other agents. The stable point of simulation is shown in Figure 8.

Figure 7: The agent on the left is approaching a conversation. Arrows indicate where the agents will move from now until the simulation stabilizes.

Figure 8: Stable point after the fourth agent joins the conversation.

4.2 Conversation splitting into two separate conversations

In this test case, we have 6 agents. After initial placement of the agents we issue a command for all the agents to form one conversation group. As a result they form a circular formation as can be seen in Figure 9.

We let the agents talk for a while and then give a command to the two agents on the right side of the group to start a side conversation. After this a complex sequence of events takes place. Initially the remaining agents still think that those two agents are part of their conversation group. They have to disambiguate the speech of those two agents and decide whether this is just an interruption or a split in the

Figure 9: Agents form in a circle to engage in a single conversation.

conversation. After a while they realize that those agents are having a separate conversation.

Deciding that the agents on the right have left the conversation leads to a change in the force field. The agents that were closest to the split are bothered by the noise and start adjusting by moving away. By doing this they change the shape of formation which causes the farther agents to also adapt back into circular formation. At the same time the agents who split also move away from the others until they get to a point where all are satisfied. The point where the simulation stabilized is shown in Figure 10.

Figure 10: After two agents leave the conversation the agents adapt to it by repositioning.

4.3 Effect of proxemics

In this test case, we examine the effects when the social zones of the agents are not compatible. This frequently happens when we have people from different cultures with a large difference in distances for social zones. An example would be North Americans compared to Arabs. Americans prefer a much greater inter-personal distance than Arabs. Empirical data shows that in many such situations there is a sort of dance with one agent moving in while another moves away (Scheflen, 1975).

Figure 11: Incompatible social zones.

Figure 11 shows an example of agents with incompatible social zones. The markings on the ground indicate the minimum and maximum acceptable distance for social zone for each agent. We can see that the agent on the left has a much smaller comfortable distance than the one on the right. In the current position the left agent feels that the other one is too far, while the right agent thinks everything is fine. This causes the left agent to make a step forward. Consequently by doing so he steps into personal zone of the right agent. Now the left agent is satisfied with the situation but the right agent feels uncomfortable and decides to take a step back to keep the other agent out of his personal zone. If nothing else intervenes, this process can continue, as the agent on the left "chases" the one on the right out of the marketplace.

5 Conclusions

In the previous section, we have shown examples of how the movement algorithm can mirror many effects we see in real conversations. The examples however were very constrained and could not show all the possible combinations that could result from random choices the agents can make. Given the fact that each agent maintains his own belief about who is currently in their conversation we can see many interesting effects when those beliefs become unsynchronized.

As seen in the third test case, we can get some very interesting results when we simulate agents of different cultures. We think that this simulation approach can be fruitful for modeling cultural differences in conversational behavior, and could be used for inter-cultural and cross-cultural awareness and training. We are currently exploring whether we can model different cultural norms for conversational behaviors in ways such that the resulting agent interaction can be recognized as appropriate to one culture or another.

There are still several improvements possible for the conversation simulation. On the presentation side we are planning to make some improvements to the bodies and number and types of conversational gestures they can display. We also plan to improve the algorithm so that it will be able to generate different conversation styles. Currently all conversations take the same form where all the agents have the same goals, their only goal is to engage in conversation with other agents. We plan to introduce the notion of tasks so that we can better simulate different kinds of activities such as asking for directions, a political debate, or casual conversation.

Acknowledgments

The project described here has been sponsored by the U.S. Army Research, Development, and Engineering Command (RDECOM). Statements and opinions expressed do not necessarily reflect the position or the policy of the United States Government, and no official endorsement should be inferred.

References

Jeremy N. Bailenson, Jim Blascovich, Andrew C. Beall, and Jack M. Loomis. 2003. Interpersonal distance in immersive virtual environments. *Personality and Social Psychology Bulletin*, 29:819–833.

Justine Cassell, Joseph Sullivan, Scott Prevost, and Elizabeth Churchill, editors. 2000. *Embodied Conversational Agents*. MIT Press, Cambridge, MA.

Edward T. Hall. 1968. Proxemics. *Current Anthropology*, 9(2/3):83–108, apr.

Dirk Helbing and Péter Molnár. 1995. Social force model for pedestrian dynamics. *Phys. Rev. E*, 51(5):4282–4286, May.

Dusan Jan and David R. Traum. 2005. Dialog simulation for background characters. *Lecture Notes in Computer Science*, pages 65–74.

Adam Kendon, 1990. *Spatial Organization in Social Encounters: the F-formation System*, pages 209–237. Cambridge University Press.

E. Padilha and J. Carletta. 2002. A simulation of small group discussion. *Proceedings of EDILOG 2002: Sixth Workshop on the Semantics and Pragmatics of Dialogue*, pages 117–124.

Matthias Rehm, Elisabeth Andre, and Michael Nischt. 2005. Let's come together - social navigation behaviors of virtual and real humans. In Mark Maybury et al., editor, *INTETAIN 2005*, LNAI, pages 122–131. Springer.

Albert E. Scheflen. 1975. Micro-territories in human interaction. In Adam Kendon, Richard M. Harris, and Mary Ritchie Key, editors, *World Anthropology: Organization of Behavior in Face-to-Face Interaction*, pages 159–173. Mouton, Paris.

Wei Shao and Demetri Terzopoulos. 2005. Autonomous pedestrians. In *SCA '05: Proceedings of the 2005 ACM SIGGRAPH/Eurographics symposium on Computer animation*, pages 19–28, New York, NY, USA. ACM Press.

G. Keith Still. 2000. *Crowd Dynamics*. Ph.D. thesis, Warwick University.

Mankyu Sung, Michael Gleicher, and Stephen Chenney. 2004. Scalable behaviors for crowd simulation. *Computer Graphics Forum*, 23(3):519–528.

Hannes Hogni Vilhjalmsson and Justine Cassell. 1998. Bodychat: autonomous communicative behaviors in avatars. In *AGENTS '98: Proceedings of the second international conference on Autonomous agents*, pages 269–276, New York, NY, USA. ACM Press.

Design and validation of ECA gestures to improve dialogue system robustness

Beatriz López, Álvaro Hernández, David Díaz, Rubén Fernández, Luis Hernández
GAPS, Signal, Systems and Radiocommunications Department
Universidad Politécnica de Madrid
Ciudad Universitaria s/n, 28040 Madrid, Spain
alvaro@gaps.ssr.upm.es

Doroteo Torre
ATVS, Escuela Politécnica Superior
Universidad Autónoma de Madrid
Ciudad Universitaria de Cantoblanco, 28049 Madrid, Spain
Doroteo.torre@uam.es

Abstract

In this paper we present validation tests that we have carried out on gestures that we have designed for an embodied conversational agent (ECAs), to assess their soundness with a view to applying said gestures in a forthcoming experiment to explore the possibilities ECAs can offer to overcome typical robustness problems in spoken language dialogue systems (SLDSs). The paper is divided into two parts: First we carry our a literature review to acquire a sense of the extent to which ECAs can help overcome user frustration during human-machine interaction. Then we associate tentative, yet specific, ECA gestural behaviour with each of the main dialogue stages, with special emphasis on problem situations. In the second part we describe the tests we have carried out to validate our ECA's gestural repertoire. The results obtained show that users generally understand and naturally accept the gestures, to a reasonable degree. This encourages us to proceed with the next stage of research: evaluating the gestural strategy in real dialogue situations with the aim of learning about how to favour a more efficient and pleasant dialogue flow for the users.

1 Introduction

Spoken language dialogue systems and embodied conversational agents are being introduced in a rapidly increasing number of Human-Computer Interaction (HCI) applications. The technologies involved in SLDSs (speech recognition, dialogue design, etc.) are mature enough to allow the creation of trustworthy applications. However, robustness problems still arise in concrete limited dialogue systems because there are many error sources that may cause the system to perform poorly. A common example is that users tend to repeat their previous utterance with some frustration when error recovery mechanisms come into play, which does not help the recognition process, and as a result using the system seems slow and unnatural (Boyce, 1999).

At the same time, embodied conversational agents (ECAs) are gaining prominence in HCI systems, since they make for more user-friendly applications while increasing communication effectiveness. There are many studies on the effects – from psychological to efficiency in goal achievement– ECAs have on users of a variety of applications, see Bickmore et al. (2004) and Brave et al. (2005), but still very few (Bell and Gustafson, 2003) on the impact of ECAs in directed dialogue situations where robustness is a problem.

Our research explores the potential of ECAs to assist in, or resolve, certain difficult dialogue situations that have been identified by various leading authors in the field (Cassell and Thorisson, 1999; Cassell and Stone, 1999), as well as a few we our-

Proceedings of the Workshop on Embodied Language Processing, pages 67–74,
Prague, Czech Republic, June 28, 2007.

selves suggest. After identifying the problematic situations of the dialogue we suggest a gestural strategy for the ECA to respond to such problem situations. Then we propose an experimental framework, for forthcoming tests, to study the potential benefits of adding nonverbal communication in complex dialogue situations. In the study we present here we focus on preliminary validation of our gestural repertoire through user tests. We conclude by presenting our results and suggesting the direction our research will take from this point.

2 How ECA technology can improve interaction with SLDSs

There are many nonverbal elements of communication in everyday life that are important because they convey a considerable amount of information and qualify the spoken message, sometimes even to the extent that what is meant is actually the opposite of what is said (Krauss et al., 1996). ECAs offer the possibility to combine several communication modes such as speech and gestures, making it possible, in theory, to create interfaces with which human-machine interaction is much more natural and comfortable. In fact, they are already being employed to improve interaction (Massaro et al., 2000).

These are some common situations with SLDSs in which an ECA could have a positive effect:

Efficient turn management: The body language and expressiveness of agents are important not only to reinforce the spoken message, but also to regulate the flow of the dialogue, as Cassell points out (in Bickmore et al., 2004).

Improving error recovery: The process of recognition error recovery usually leads to a certain degree of user frustration (see Oviatt and VanGent, 1996). Indeed, it is common, once an error occurs, to enter into an error spiral in which the system is trying to recover, the user gets ever more frustrated, and this frustration interferes in the recognition process making the situation worse (Oviatt et al., 1998). ECAs may help reduce frustration, and by doing so make error recovery more effective (Hone, 2005).

Correct understanding of the state of the dialogue: Sometimes the user doesn't know whether or not things are going normally (Oviatt, 1994). This sometimes leads the dialogue to error states that could be avoided. The expressive capacity of ECAs could be used to reflect with greater clarity the state the system takes the dialogue to be in.

3 Suggesting ECA behaviour for each dialogue situation

A variety of studies have been carried out on behavioural strategies for embodied conversational agents (Poggi, 2001; Cassell et al., 2000; Cassell et al., 2001; Chovil, 1992; Kendon, 1990), which deal with behaviour in hypothetical situations and in terms of the informational goals of each particular interaction (be it human-human or human-machine). We direct our attention to the overall dialogue systems dynamics, focussing specifically on typical robustness problems and how to favour smooth sailing through the different stages of the dialogue. We draw from existing research undertaken to try to understand the effects different gestures displayed by ECAs have on people, and we apply this knowledge to a real dialogue system. In Table 1 we show the basic set of gestures we are using as a starting point. They are based mainly on descriptions in Bickmore (et al., 2004) and Cassell (et al., 2000), and on recommendations in Cassell and Thorisson (1999), Cassell (et al., 2001), Chovil (1992), Kendon (1990) and San-Segundo (et al., 2001), to which we have added a few suggestions of our own.

Dialogue stage	ECA behaviour (movements, gestures and other cues)
Initiation (welcoming the user)	1. Welcome message: look at the camera, smile, wave hand 2. Explanation of the task: zoom in 3. Zoom out, lights dim
Give turn	Look directly at the user, raise eyebrows. Camera zooms out. Lights dim.
Take turn	Look directly at the user, raise hands into gesture space. Camera zooms in. Light gets brighter.
Wait	Slight leaning back, one arm crossed and the other touching the cheek shift of body weight
Help	Beat gesture with the hands. Change of posture
Error recovery with correction	Lean towards the camera, beat gesture
Confirmation (high confidence)	Nod, smile, eyes fully open
Confirmation (low confidence)	Slight leaning of the head to one side, stop smiling, mildly squint

Table 1: Gesture repertoire for the main dialogue stages

3.1 Initiation

The inclusion of an ECA at this stage "humanises" the system (Oviatt and Adams, 2000). This is a problem, first because once a user has such high expectations the system can only end up disappointing her, and secondly because the user will tend to use more natural (and thus complex) communication, which the system is unable to handle, and the experience will ultimately be frustrating.

On the other hand, especially in the case of new users, contact with a dialoguing animated character may have the effect that the user's level of attention to the actual information that is being given is reduced (Schaumburg, 2001; Catrambone, 2002). Thus the goal is to present a human-like interface that is, at the same time, less striking and thus less distracting at first contact, and one that clearly "sets the rules" of the interaction and makes sure that the user keeps it framed within the capability of the system.

We have designed a welcome gesture for our ECA based on the recommendations in Kendon (1990), to test whether or not it fosters a sense of ease in the user and helps her concentrate on the task at hand. Playing with the zoom, the size and the position of the ECA on the screen may also prove to be useful to frame the communication better (see Table 1).

3.2 Turn Management

Turn management involves two basic actions: taking turn and giving turn. Again, in Table 1 we show the corresponding ECA gestures we will start testing with. Note that apart from the ECA gestures, we also play with zoom and light intensity: when it's the ECA's turn to speak the camera zooms-in slightly and the light becomes brighter, and when it's the user's turn the camera zooms out and the lights dim. The idea is that, hopefully, the user will associate each camera shot and level of light intensity with each of the turn modes, and so know when she is expected to speak.

The following are some typical examples of problem situations together with further considerations about ECA behaviour that could help avoid or recover from them:

- The user tries to interrupt at a point at which the barge-in feature is not active. If this happens the system does not process what the user has said, and when the system finally returns to listening mode there is silence from both parts: the system expects input from the user, and the user expects an answer. Often both finally break the silence at the same time and the cycle begins again, or, if the system caught part of the user's utterance, a recognition error will most likely occur and the system will fall into a recognition error recovery subdialogue that the user does not expect. To help avoid such faulty events the ECAs demeanour should indicate as clearly as possible that the user is not being listened to at that particular moment. Speaking while looking away, perhaps at some object, and absence of attention cues (such as nodding) are possible ways to show that the user is not expected to interrupt the ECA. Since our present dialogue system produces fairly short utterances for the ECA, we are somewhat limited as to the active strategies to build into the ECA's behaviour. However, there are at least three cues the user could read to realise that the system didn't listen to what she said. The first is the fact that the system carries on speaking, ignoring the user's utterance. Second, at the end of the system's turn the ECA will perform a specific give-turn gesture. And third, after giving the turn the ECA will remain still and silent for a few seconds before performing a waiting gesture (leaning back slightly with her arms crossed, shifting the body weight from one leg to another; see Table 1). In addition, if the user still remains silent after yet another brief waiting period the system will offer help. It will be interesting to see at which point users realise that the system didn't register their utterance.
- A similar situation occurs if the Voice Activity Detector (VAD) fails and the system doesn't capture the user's entire utterance, or when the user simply doesn't say anything when she is expected to ("no input"). Again, both system and user end up waiting for each other to say something. And again, the strategy we use is to have the ECA display a waiting posture.
- It can also happen that the user doesn't speak but the VAD "thinks" she did, perhaps after detecting some background noise

(a "phantom input"). The dialogue system's reaction to something the user didn't say can cause surprise and confusion in the user. Here the visible reactions of an ECA might help the user understand what has happened and allow her to steer the dialogue back on track.

3.3 Recognition Confidence Scheme

Once the user utterance has been recognised, information confirmation strategies are commonly used in dialogue systems. Different strategies are taken depending on the level of confidence in the correctness of the user locution as captured by the speech recognition unit (San-Segundo et al., 2001). Our scheme is as follows:

- *High confidence:* if recognition confidence is high enough to safely assume that no error has occurred, the dialogue strategy is made more fluent, with no confirmations being sought by the system.
- *Intermediate confidence:* the result is regarded as uncertain and the system tries implicit confirmation (by including the uncertain piece of information in a question about something else.) This, combined with a mixed initiative approach, allows the user to correct the system if an error did occur.
- *Low confidence:* in this case recognition has probably failed. When this happens the dialogue switches to a more guided strategy, with explicit confirmation of the collected information and no mixed initiative. The user's reply may confirm that the system understood correctly, in which case the dialogue continues to flow normally, or, on the other hand, it may show that there was a recognition error. In this case an error recovery mechanism begins.

In addition to the dialogue strategies, ECAs could also be used to reflect in their manner the level of confidence that the system has understood the user, in accordance with the confirmation dialogue strategies. While the user speaks, our ECA will, if the recognition confidence level is high, nod her head (Cassell et al., 2000), smile and have her eyes fully open to give the user feedback that everything is going well and the system is understanding. If, on the other hand, confidence is low, in order to make it clearer to the user that there might be some problem with recognition and that extra care should be taken, an option might be for the ECA to gesture in such a way as to show that she isn't quite sure she's understood but is making an effort to. We have attempted to create this effect by having the ECA lean her head slightly to one side, stop smiling and mildly squint. Our goal, once again, is to find out whether these cues do indeed help users realise what the situation is. This is especially important if it helps to avoid the well-known problem of falling into error spirals when a recognition error occurs in a spoken dialogue system (Bulyko et al., 2005). In the case of intermediate recognition confidence followed by a mixed initiative strategy involving implicit confirmation, specific gestures could also be envisaged. We have chosen not to include specific gestures for these situations in our first trials, however, so as not to obscure our observations for the high and low confidence cases. A neutral stance for the intermediate confidence level should be a useful reference against which to compare the other two cases.

3.4 Recognition Problems

We will consider those situations in which the system finds the user's utterance incomprehensible (no-match situations) and those in which the system gets the user's message wrong (recognitions errors). When a no-match occurs there are two ways in which an ECA can be useful. First, what the character should say must be carefully pondered to ensure that the user is aware that the system didn't understand what she said and that the immediate objective is to solve this particular problem. This knowledge can make the user more patient with the system and tolerate better the unexpected lengthening of the interaction (Goldberg, 2003). Second, the ECAs manner should try to keep the user in a positive attitude. A common problem in no-match and error recovery situations is that the user becomes irritated or hyperarticulates in an attempt to make herself understood, which in fact increases the probability of yet another no-match or a recognition error. This we should obviously try to avoid.

The ECA behaviour strategy we will test in no-match situations is to have the character lean towards the camera and raise her eyebrows (the idea being to convey a sense of surprise coupled with friendly interest). We have based our gesture on one given in (Fagerberg et al., 2003). If the user points out to the system that there has been a recognition error in a way that gives the correct information at the same time, then the ECA will confirm the corrected information with special emphasis in speech and gesture. For this purpose we have designed a beat gesture with both hands (see Table 1).

3.5 Help offers and request

It will be interesting to see whether the fact that help is offered by an animated character (the ECA) is regarded by users to be more user-friendly than otherwise. If users feel more comfortable with the ECA, perhaps they will show greater initiative in requesting help from the system; and when it is offered by the system (when a problem situation occurs), the presence of a friendly ECA might help control user frustration. While the ECA is giving the requested information, she will perform a beat gesture with both hands for emphasis, and she will also change posture. The idea is to see whether this captures the interest of the user, makes her more confident and the experience more pleasant or, on the contrary, it distracts the user and makes help delivery less effective.

Figure 1 illustrates a dialogue sequence including the association between the different dialogue strategies and the ECA gesture sequences after a user's utterance.

4 Experimental set up

Gestures and nonverbal communication are culture-dependent. This is an important fact to take into account because a single gesture might be interpreted in different ways depending on the user's culture (Kleinsmith et al., 2006). Therefore, a necessary step prior to the evaluation of the various hypotheses put forward in the previous section is to test the gestures we have implemented for our ECA, within the framework designed for our study. This implies validating the gestures for Spanish users, since we have based them on studies within the Anglo-Saxon culture.

4.1 Procedure

For the purpose of testing the gesture repertoire developed for our ECA we have conceived an evaluation environment that simulates a realistic mobile videotelephony application that allows users to remotely check the state (*e.g.*, on/off) of several household devices (lights, heating, etc.). Our dialogue system incorporates mixed initiative, error recovery subdialogues, context-dependent help and the production of guided or flexible dialogues according to the confidence levels of the speech recogniser. Our environment uses Nuance Communications' speech recognition technology (www.nuance.com). The ECA character has been designed by Haptek (www.haptek.com).

During the gesture validation tests users didn't interact directly with the dialogue system. We first asked the users to watch a system simulator (a video recording of a user interacting with the system), so that they could see the ECA performing the gestures in the context of a real dialogue.

After watching the simulation the users were asked to fill out a questionnaire. The questionnaire allowed users to view isolated clips of each

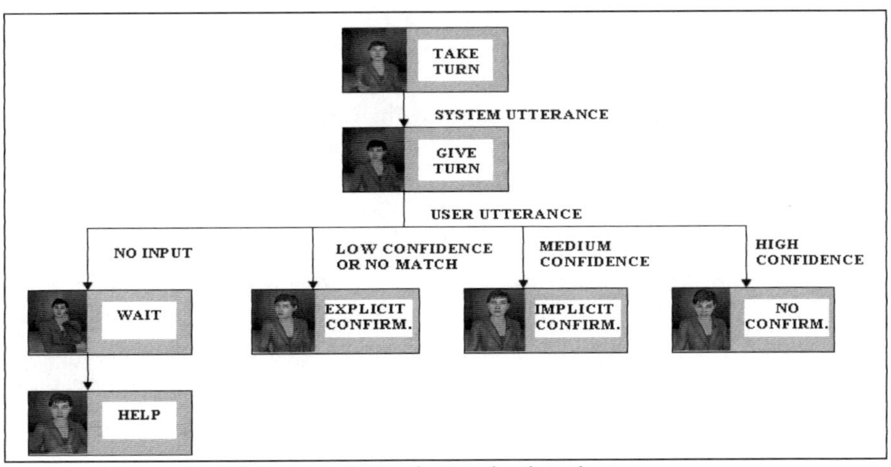

Figure 1: Dialogue strategies and related gesture sequence

of the dialogue gestures (the eight that had appeared in the video). To each gesture clip were associated questions basically covering the following three aspects:

- *Gesture interpretation*: Users are asked to interpret each gesture, choosing one from among several given options (the same options for all gestures). The aim is to see whether the meaning and intention of each gesture are clear. In addition users told us whether they thought they had seen the gesture in the previous dialogue sample.
- *Gesture design:* Do users think the gesture is well made and does it look natural? To answer this question we asked users to rate the quality, expressiveness and clarity of the ECAs gesture (on a 9-point Likert scale).
- *User expectations*: Users rated how useful they thought each gesture was (on a 9-point Likert scale). The idea is to juxtapose the utility function of the gestures in the users' mental model to our own when we designed them, and evaluate the similarity. In addition we collected suggestions as to how the users thought the gestures could be improved.

4.2 Results

We recruited 17 test users (most of them students between 20 and 25 years of age) for our trial. The results concerning the three previously mentioned aspects are shown in Table 2. In the case of the *gesture interpretation*, we present the percentage of the users who interpreted each gesture "correctly" (*i.e.*, as we had intended when we designed them). Depending on this percentage we label each gesture as "Good", "Average", or "Bad". For each of the parameters for *gesture design* and *user expectations* we give the mean and the standard deviation of the Likert scale scores. We label the average scores as "Low" (Likert score between 1 and 3), Medium (4-6) or "High" (7-9).

We now discuss the results separately for each of the dimensions:

Regarding user expectations, the values for each gesture are High except for two of them, valued as Medium. These two gestures are the welcome gesture and the gesture for offering help. In the case of the welcome gesture, users probably believe the beginning of the dialogue is already well enough defined when the ECA starts to speak. If so, users might see an element of redundancy in the welcome gesture, lowering its perceived utility in the dialogue process. On the other hand, the help gesture utility might be valued lower than the rest because many users didn't seem to understand its purpose (the clarity of the Help gesture was the least valued of all, μ=5.117). Nevertheless, the general user impressions of the utility of the evaluated gesture repertoire fairly high.

In relation to gesture design, we can see that, overall, the marks for quality and expressiveness are high. This implies our gesture design is, on the whole, adequate. Regarding the clarity of the gestures, three of them are valued as Medium. These are the gestures expressing Give Turn, Error Recovery and Help offer. This could be related to the prevailing opinion among users that there are a few confusing gestures, although they are better understood in the context of the application, when you listen to what the ECA says.

Only half of the gestures were properly interpreted by the users. Those that weren't (Give Turn, Take Turn, Error Recovery and the Help gesture) are, we realize, the subtlest in the repertoire, so we asked ourselves if there could be relation between a bad interpretation of the gesture and the whether that user didn't remember seeing the gesture in the dialogue. In Figure 2 we show the number of users who claimed they hadn't seen the ECA gestures during the dialogue sample. The coloured bars represent the overall accuracy in the interpretation of the gesture. We may observe that the gestures that a larger number of users hadn't seen in the dialogue, and therefore, hadn't an image of in proper context, tended also to be considered more unclear.

We may conclude that some gestures need to be evaluated in context. In any case, and in spite of the uncertainty we have found regarding the interpretation of certain gestures, we believe the positive evaluation by the users for the expressiveness and the quality of the gestures justifies us in validating our gestural repertoire for the next research stage where we will evaluate how well our ECA gestures function under real interaction conditions (taking into account objective data related to dialogue efficiency).

	INTERPRETATION	DESIGN			EXPECTATIONS
	Good Interpretation (%)	**Quality**	**Clarity**	**Expressiveness**	**Usefulness**
G1 Wellcome	88.23 Good	7.117 (0.927) High	7.588 (1.277) High	6.764 (1.147) High	5.647 (2.119) Medium
G2 Give Turn	35.29 Average	6.647 (1.057) High	5.823 (1.333) Medium	6.470 (1.007) High	6.588 (1.543) High
G3 Take Turn	23.53 Bad	7.117 (1.166) High	6.705 (1.447) High	6.941 (1.444) High	6.647 (1.271) High
G4 Wait	82.35 Good	7.058 (1.088) High	7.176 (1.185) High	7.176 (0.727) High	6.588 (1.622) High
G5 Confirmation (Low confidence)	76.47 Good	8.294 (0.587) High	8.058 (1.028) High	8.058 (1.028) High	7.941 (1.028) High
G6 Confirmation (High confidence)	94.11 Good	7.529 (1.124) High	7.529 (1.124) High	7.705(1.263) High	7.588 (1.175) High
G7 Error Recovery	41.17 Average	6.941 (1.088) High	5.588 (2.032) Medium	6.529 (1.462) High	6.058 (1.390) High
G8 Help	35.29 Average	6.823 (1.185) High	5.117 (1.932) Medium	6.058(1.560) High	5.529 (1.771) Medium

Table 2: Results of the gesture validation tests.

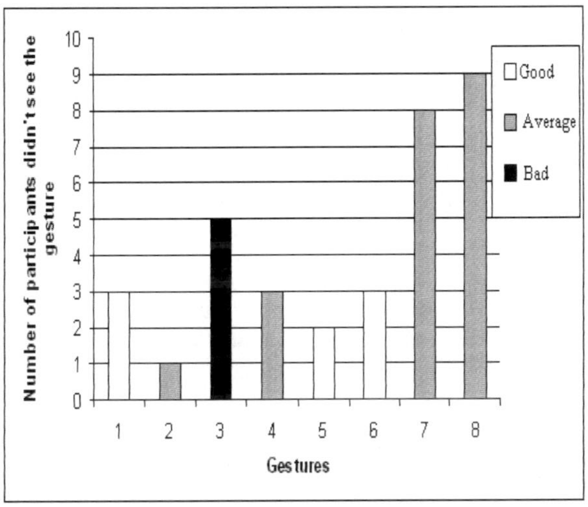

Figure 2: Interpretation vs. 'visibility' of the gestures.

5 Conclusions and future lines of work

In this article we have identified a range of problem situations that may arise in dialogue systems, and defined various strategies for using an ECA to improve user-machine interaction throughout the whole dialogue. We have developed an experimental set up for a user validation of ECA gestures in the dialogue system and have obtained quantitative results and user opinions to improve the design of the gestures. The results of this validation allow us to be in a position to begin testing our dialogue system and evaluate our ECA gestures in the context of a real dialogue.

In future experiments we will attempt to go one step further and analyse how empathic emotions vs. self-oriented behaviour (see Brave et al., 2005) may affect the resolution of a variety of dialogue situations. To this end we plan to design ECA prototypes that incorporate specific emotions, hoping to learn how best to connect empathically with the user, and what effects this may have on dialogue dynamics and the overall user perception of the system.

References

Linda Bell and Joakim Gustafson, 2003. *Child and Adult SpeakerAdaptation during Error Resolution in a Publicly Available Spoken Dialogue System.* Proceedings of Eurospeech 03, Geneve, Schweiz.

Timothy W. Bickmore, Justine Cassell, Jan van Kuppevelt, Laila Dybkjaer and Niels Ole Bernsen, 2004. *Natural, Intelligent and Effective Interaction with Multimodal Dialogue Systems*, chapter Social Dialogue with Embodied Conversational Agents. Kluwer Academic.

Susan J. Boyce, 1999. *Spoken natural language dialogue systems: user interface issues for the future.* In Human Factors and Voice Interactive Systems. D. Gardner-Bonneau Ed. Norwell, Massachusetts, Kluwer Academic Publishers: 37-62.

Scott Brave, Clifford Nass, Kevin Hutchinson, 2005. *Computers that care: investigating the effects of ori-*

entation of emotion exhibited by an embodied computer agent. Int. J. Human-Computer Studies, Nr. 62, Issue 2, pp. 161-178.

Ivan Bulyko, Katrin Kirchhoff, Mari Ostendorf, Julie Goldberg, 2005 *Error correction detection and response generation in a spoken dialogue system.* Speech Communication 45, 271-288.

Justine Cassell, Kristinn R. Thorisson, 1999. *The power of a nod and aglance: envelope vs. emotional feedback in animated conversational agents.* Applied Artificial Intelligence, vol.13, pp.519-538.

Justine Cassell and Matthew Stone, 1999. *Living Hand to Mouth: Psychological Theories about Speech and Gesture in Interactive Dialogue Systems.* Proceedings of the AAAI 1999 Fall Symposium on Psychological Models of Communication in Collaborative Systems, pp. 34-42. November 5-7, North Falmouth, MA, 1999.

Justine Cassell, Timothy W. Bickmore, Hannes Vilhjálmsson and Hao Yan, 2000. *More than just a pretty face: affordances of embodiment.* In Proceedings of the 5th international Conference on intelligent User interfaces.

Justine Cassell, Yukiko I. Nakano, Timothy W. Bickmore, Candace L. Sidner and Charles Rich, 2001. *Non-verbal cues for discourse structure.* In Proceedings of the 39th Annual Meeting on Association For Computational Linguistics.

Richard Catrambone, 2002 *Anthropomorphic agents as a user interface paradigm: Experimental findings and a framework for research.* In: Proceedings of the 24th Annual Conference of the Cognitive Science Society (pp. 166-171), Fairfax, VA, August.

Nicole Chovil, 1992. *Discourse-Oriented Facial Displays in Conversation.* Research on Language and Social Interaction, 25, 163-194.

Petra Fagerberg, Anna Ståhl, Kristina Höök, 2003. *Designing Gestures for Afective Input: an Analysis of Shape, Effort and Valence.* In Proceedings of Mobile Ubiquitious and Multimedia, Norrköping, Sweden.

Julie Goldberg, Mari Ostendorf, Katrin Kirchhoff, 2003. *The impact of response wording in error correction subdialogs,* In EHSD-2003, 101-106.

Kate Hone, 2005. *Animated Agents to reduce user frustration,* in The 19th British HCI Group Annual Conference, Edinburgh, UK.

Adam Kendon, 1990. *Conducting interaction: patterns of behaviour in focused encounters,* Cambridge University Press.

Andrea Kleinsmith, P. Ravindra De Silva, Nadia Bianchi-Berthouze, 2006 *Cross-cultural differences in recognizing affect from body posture* Interacting with computers 10 1371-1389

Robert M. Krauss, Yihsiu Chen and Purnima Chawla, 1996 *Nonverbal behavior and nonverbal communication: What do conversational hand gestures tell us?* In M. Zanna (Ed.), Advances in experimental social psychology (pp. 389 450).San Diego, CA: Academic Press.

Dominic W. Massaro, Michael M. Cohen, Jonas Beskow and Ronald A. Cole, 2000.*Developing and evaluating conversational agents.* In Embodied Conversational Agents MIT Press, Cambridge, MA, 287-318.

Sharon Oviatt. 1994. *Interface techniques for minimizing disfluent input to spoken language systems.* In Proc. CHI'94 (pp. 205-210) Boston, ACM Press, 1994

Sharon Oviatt and Robert VanGent, 1996, *Error resolution duringmultimodal humancomputer interaction.* Proc. International Conference on Spoken Language Processing, 1 204-207.

Sharon Oviatt, Margaret MacEachern, and Gina-Anne Levow, G.,1998. *Predicting hyperarticulate speech during human-computer error resolution.* Speech Communication, vol.24, 2, 1-23.

Sharon Oviatt, and Bridget Adams, 2000. *Designing and evaluating conversational interfaces with animated characters.* Embodied conversational agents, MIT Press: 319-345.

Isabella Poggi, 2001. *How to decide which gesture to make according to our goals and our contextual knowledge.* Paper presented at Gesture Workshop 2001 London 18th-20th April, 2001

Ruben San-Segundo, Juan M. Montero, Javier Ferreiros, Ricardo Córdoba, Jose M. Pardo, 2001 *Designing Confirmation Mechanisms and Error Recover Techniques in a Railway Information System for Spanish.* SIGDIAL. Septiembre 1-2, Aalborg (Dinamarca).

Heike Schaumburg, 2001. *Computers as tools or as social actors?the users' perspective on anthropomorphic agents.*International Journal of Cooperative Information Systems.10, 1, 2, 217-234.

Author Index